CAMBRIDGE LIBRARY COLLECTION

Books of enduring scholarly value

Religion

For centuries, scripture and theology were the focus of prodigious amounts of scholarship and publishing, dominated in the English-speaking world by the work of Protestant Christians. Enlightenment philosophy and science, anthropology, ethnology and the colonial experience all brought new perspectives, lively debates and heated controversies to the study of religion and its role in the world, many of which continue to this day. This series explores the editing and interpretation of religious texts, the history of religious ideas and institutions, and not least the encounter between religion and science.

Confucianism and Modern China

The British colonial administrator and scholar Sir Reginald Fleming Johnston (1874–1938) travelled extensively in the Far East, developing a deep interest in Chinese culture and spirituality. His fourteen-year posting to the relatively quiet port of Weihaiwei allowed him to indulge this interest and to travel to places not usually visited by Europeans. Well acquainted with the philosophy of Confucius, Johnston had happily quoted the Confucian classics in his court judgments at Weihaiwei. In 1918, he was appointed tutor to the young Puyi (1906–67), who had been China's last emperor before his forced abdication. This 1934 publication, developed from lectures, presents an accessible interpretation of the tenets and fortunes of Confucianism, notably the impact of the New Culture Movement on the philosophy's place in Chinese society. Among other works, Johnston's *Buddhist China* (1913) and *Twilight in the Forbidden City* (1934) are also reissued in this series.

Cambridge University Press has long been a pioneer in the reissuing of out-of-print titles from its own backlist, producing digital reprints of books that are still sought after by scholars and students but could not be reprinted economically using traditional technology. The Cambridge Library Collection extends this activity to a wider range of books which are still of importance to researchers and professionals, either for the source material they contain, or as landmarks in the history of their academic discipline.

Drawing from the world-renowned collections in the Cambridge University Library and other partner libraries, and guided by the advice of experts in each subject area, Cambridge University Press is using state-of-the-art scanning machines in its own Printing House to capture the content of each book selected for inclusion. The files are processed to give a consistently clear, crisp image, and the books finished to the high quality standard for which the Press is recognised around the world. The latest print-on-demand technology ensures that the books will remain available indefinitely, and that orders for single or multiple copies can quickly be supplied.

The Cambridge Library Collection brings back to life books of enduring scholarly value (including out-of-copyright works originally issued by other publishers) across a wide range of disciplines in the humanities and social sciences and in science and technology.

Confucianism and Modern China

The Lewis Fry Memorial Lectures, 1933–34,
Delivered at Bristol University

REGINALD F. JOHNSTON

CAMBRIDGE
UNIVERSITY PRESS

CAMBRIDGE
UNIVERSITY PRESS

University Printing House, Cambridge, CB2 8BS, United Kingdom

Cambridge University Press is part of the University of Cambridge.

It furthers the University's mission by disseminating knowledge in the pursuit of
education, learning and research at the highest international levels of excellence.

www.cambridge.org
Information on this title: www.cambridge.org/9781108080361

© in this compilation Cambridge University Press 2015

This edition first published 1934
This digitally printed version 2015

ISBN 978-1-108-08036-1 Paperback

CONFUCIANISM
AND MODERN CHINA

像真聖孔刻石縣阜曲摹敬

CONFUCIUS

(This Chinese woodcut, as the inscription states, is a reproduction of
the portrait carved in stone and preserved in the great Confucian
Temple at Ch'ü-Fou, in Shantung.)

CONFUCIANISM AND MODERN CHINA

THE LEWIS FRY MEMORIAL LECTURES
1933-34
Delivered at Bristol University

by

REGINALD F. JOHNSTON
K.C.M.G., C.B.E., M.A. (Oxon), Hon. LL.D.,

Professor of Chinese in the University of
London; Head of the Department of
Languages and Cultures of the Far East
in the London School of Oriental Studies.

LONDON
VICTOR GOLLANCZ LTD
14 Henrietta Street Covent Garden
1934

Printed in Great Britain by
The Camelot Press Ltd., London and Southampton

CONTENTS

ILLUSTRATIONS

PREFACE

THE LECTURES now published in an expanded form were delivered in the Great Hall of the University of Bristol in November and December, 1933. I desire to express my thanks to the University for giving me this valued opportunity of addressing a Bristol audience on the subject of the present condition and prospects of Confucianism in China, and to my old friend, Dr. Thomas Loveday, Vice-Chancellor, for the courtesy and hospitality extended to me by him during my visit to the city and University.

REGINALD F. JOHNSTON.

The School of Oriental Studies,
London University.

CHAPTER I

INTRODUCTION

BEFORE I BEGIN TO ADDRESS YOU on the subject of Confucianism and Modern China, I am going to make a confession which, in a lecturer who presumably hopes to carry his audience with him, is perhaps as unprecedented as it is rash. I am vividly conscious of the fact that the subject which I have chosen bristles with controversial material, and it is my painful duty to give you a solemn warning against too ready an acceptance of much that I am going to say. Whatever you may think of this warning, which almost amounts to an admission of my own unworthiness to address you from this platform, it will at least show you that I am no politician. I am dismally cognisant of my own liability to err.

I must also warn you that had this been a Chinese instead of an English University I should have had to face a storm of protest before I had uttered a single word. The mere title of my lectures would of itself have been sufficient to arouse a lively spirit of antagonism in a large section of my audience. I should have been told that however prominent may have been the part that Confucianism has played in the China of the past, it has no significance for the forward-gazing

China of to-day ; that it has nothing of value
to transmit to the China of to-morrow ; and that to
link " Confucianism " with " Modern China " is therefore an undeserved honour for Confucianism and an
insult to Modern China.

These are views which I do not share ; nevertheless
they have been accepted, to a large extent, by those
whose influence is dominant in Chinese academic
circles at the present time, and they account for the
humble position now held by Confucianism in the
educational system through which the life and thought
and character of the Chinese people are being re-
moulded to-day.

In these lectures I will endeavour to justify the faith
that is in me and to explain the grounds on which I
base my belief that Confucianism is still a living force
among the Chinese people and has a message of great
value for the China of the present and future.

I have been warned that in my discussion of this
subject I must not take a general knowledge of the
Confucian system for granted, and that even a Bristol
audience will expect me to give some kind of an answer
to the question " What is Confucianism ? "

I say " even a Bristol audience," for I look on Bristol
as a city of " Merchant Venturers " in the best sense
of the term, a city of world-wide interests not exclusively
identified with trade and commerce, a city that has
devoted itself to adventurous research not only in
material things but also in things of the spirit. And if

this has been true of the Bristol of past centuries, how much more likely is it to be true of the Bristol which is now assuming an honourable place among the flourishing centres of English academic life?

If then I must attempt an answer to the question "What is Confucianism?" I have too much respect for my Bristol audience to offer it a definition of the nutshell variety. I might produce the packed nutshell, and we might open it together with the most scrupulous care, but the spirit of Confucianism would have flown.

Nor will I ask you to be satisfied with any definition, however elaborate, drawn from the Confucian researches of Western Orientalists. If it be true, as we are so often told, that only a Christian can understand and interpret Christianity, surely it is no less true that it takes a Confucian to understand and interpret Confucianism. This might be regarded as a truism were it not that many Western students of things Chinese seem to have overlooked it. We cannot appreciate the beauty of a cathedral window by looking at it from the outside. Similarly, if we wish to form an adequate idea of Confucianism we must make an effort to look at it from within, and to approximate as closely as possible to the standpoint of those who are themselves among the loyal guardians of the great Confucian heritage.[1]

I cannot think of a better method of approach to that standpoint than by telling you of a little episode which took place about twenty-five years ago and which led to the drawing-up of a carefully-selected list of some of the leading principles of Confucian ethics together with a running commentary by its compiler. That compiler was and is one of the greatest living Confucian scholars in China, one who by his great learning, and still more by reason of his fine character, has a better claim than any man I know to the honourable title of *chün-tzŭ*—the Confucian equivalent of a scholar and a gentleman.

CHAPTER II

FOURTEEN CONFUCIAN TEXTS

THERE IS IN the Dutch island of Java a very large and flourishing population of Chinese colonists. They are emigrants and the descendants of emigrants from the southern provinces of China. About the year 1908 the leading members of this Chinese community had become seriously concerned about the educational welfare of their children, who, they feared, were in grave danger, owing to their alien environment, of losing touch with the cultural traditions of their ancestral home. After lengthy deliberations on the subject they founded a Confucian Society which had for its main object the direction and supervision of the education of young Chinese colonists. Early in 1909 this Society, which soon became a very active and influential one, sent to China a deputation, headed by the chairman of the local Chinese Chamber of Commerce, for the purpose of consulting one of the leading scholars of the day on the best method of achieving the objects they had in view. The person to whom they applied was not only a rising Government official of unblemished reputation, but also a poet, an artist, an advocate of constitutional reform, and one of the most distinguished Confucian scholars in the Empire. His name, which recent political developments have made familiar to students of Far Eastern politics, was Chêng Hsiao-hsü, now prime-minister of Manchuria.[1]

From this able and accomplished native of the province of Fuhkien they obtained more than encouragement and good advice. He provided them with a little book or pamphlet of his own compilation and composition, to serve as a summary of Confucian ethics. Its name—*K'ung Chiao Hsin Pien*—may be translated " New Handbook of Confucian Teaching."[2] It consists of fourteen short passages or texts from the Confucian canon, each of which is accompanied by a brief commentary and explanation primarily intended for the guidance of school-teachers. All but one of the texts is taken from that famous repository of orthodox Confucian teaching known as the *Lun Yü*—usually rendered in English as " The Confucian Analects " or as " The Sayings of Confucius." The remaining one—and characteristically it takes precedence of all the others—is from the *Hsiao Ching* or " Classic of Filial Piety."

The fourteen selected texts would hardly occupy, if strung together, more than two or three quarto pages. I propose to give you my own translations of these texts together with explanatory observations, some of which will be based on the running commentary of Chêng Hsiao-hsü himself.

It is perhaps unnecessary to warn you that the fourteen texts must not be regarded as the Confucian equivalent of a creed, or as an adequate presentation of Confucian thought. Much is omitted that a European,

versed in Confucian lore, would certainly have included ; and it includes some texts that he would have
omitted as of secondary importance. Nevertheless it
may be said that this little anthology embodies sound
Confucian teaching as far as it goes, and is regarded as
applicable to the ethical and educational needs of the
present day. The texts, as I have said, were deliberately
chosen by a highly competent Chinese authority as
suitable nourishment for the minds of young Chinese
whose parents wished their education to be conducted
on strict Confucian lines and yet adapted to the needs
of the modern environment in which they would have
to spend their lives. So whatever you may think of the
anthology, you will at least have the satisfaction of
knowing that it contains nothing that is not un-
adulterated Confucianism as it is understood by a
scholar who combined loyalty to Confucius with a
modern outlook, and who did not allow his reverence
for the past to blind him to the practical needs of a
generation which, both in China and elsewhere, is
brought into unavoidable contact with a non-Chinese
environment.

Chêng Hsiao-hsü's little book was immediately
accepted by the Chinese schools of Java, and it also
received a warm welcome from large numbers of public
and private schools in China. It is now seldom or never
seen in Government schools, because the anti-Confucian educational policy of recent revolutionary
Governments in China has deprived the Confucian
classics of their place of honour in the Chinese educational system ; but it is known and valued in countless

private families in which the name of Confucius is still
held in greater honour than that of the official Sage
of Republican China—Sun Yat-sen. The latest edition
of it was published a few months ago. As Chêng
Hsiao-hsŭ states in a postscript to this edition, it was
published at my own request in order that it might
be used as a text-book by European students of Chinese
in the University of London.

The first of the texts—that from the *Classic of Filial
Piety*—consists of an utterance attributed to Confucius,
and it is introduced by the hallowed and time-honoured
phrase *Chih Shêng Hsien Shih K'ung Tzŭ Yüeh*—" The
Supreme Sage and Teacher, our Master K'ung, spoke
thus." Most of the subsequent texts are similarly introduced by the shorter formula " the Master said." In
my translation of the texts this introductory phrase
will be omitted.

I. *It is in accordance with the nature of things that of all
    beings on earth Man is the noblest.*[3]

This text may be compared with the more striking
words of Goethe—" Man is the first speech that
Nature holds with God."

In his commentary on the text, Chêng Hsiao-hsü
points out that the *shêng-jên* or Sage is only a man
among other men. Confucius himself, though a Sage
and a pre-eminent one, belongs to the same order of
being as the simplest and least advanced of mankind ;
and the ordinary man may, by strenuous endeavour,
render himself worthy of his status as the potential
equal of the Sage. This is no " modernism " but is
strictly orthodox Confucian teaching.[4]

Man's nature, the commentator continues, is such that he is capable of leading the good life. If he falls into evil ways it is not through any defect in the nature with which he came into the world ; it is because he has failed to recognise or to exercise the privileges and potentialities which were his in virtue of his manhood, and because he has *shih ch'i pên hsing*—" lost his own nature." The true follower of Confucius, says Chêng Hsiao-hsü, has a clear knowledge of his own honourable status with its rights and responsibilities, and is therefore able to bear the world's insults and injuries with equanimity. It is only the " small man " (*hsiao jên*) who, having an ignoble view of his own nature, sinks under misfortune or ill-treatment. Moreover, the true Confucian puts no faith in the alleged promises or threats of divine beings. " Foreign religions " (*wai chiao*) try to frighten " small men " out of evil-doing, and induce ignorant people to worship supernatural beings in the hope of attaining heaven or avoiding hell. This, he says, is grievous error.

I should explain that Christianity is nowhere specifically mentioned in Chêng Hsiao-hsü's booklet, the general tendency of which is in no way anti-Christian. Nevertheless the view that man must follow virtue for its own sake and not through fear of punishment or hope of reward in another world, is so characteristic of Confucian teaching that we can hardly complain of the explicit rejection of what were assumed to be the contrary teachings of " foreign religions." It is probable that under the head of " foreign religions " Chêng Hsiao-hsü included not

Bc

only Christianity but also Buddhism ; for in the so-called " Pure Land " school of Buddhism the doctrine of salvation by faith is just as prominent as it is in Christianity. There are no pictures of heaven or purgatory, or of divine saviours, to be found in Confucian books or on the walls of Confucian temples. To find these we must visit Taoist or Buddhist temples or consult the popular tracts which the priests and monks of those cults distribute among the unlettered multitude.

The Dean of St. Paul's tells us in his great work on Plotinus that " the notion that virtue is hereafter rewarded by pleasure and comfort, while vice is chastised by torments, is repugnant to the later Platonism. Plotinus says severely that if any man desires from a virtuous life anything beyond itself, it is not a virtuous life that he desires."[5] It is interesting to note that while Plotinus and the Alexandrian School were teaching this doctrine in the third century of our era, doctors of the Confucian School were teaching it simultaneously in China, where, indeed, it had been familiar for centuries.[6]

II. *When you meet with men of noble character, try to emulate them ; when you meet with inferior men, look inward and examine yourself.*[7]

This seems to require little comment. Chêng Hsiao-hsü points out that unless we strive to equal those whose moral superiority we recognise, we shall be in danger of falling to the level of those who are our moral inferiors. The true follower of Confucius, he says, is capable of distinguishing between good and evil, and exercises his moral freedom (Confucianism holds that this is his birthright) by choosing the good and eschewing the evil. It is not enough to try to model ourselves on the good men of ancient times or to study the books they have left us ; we are obliged to come into daily contact with men of our own time, and we must therefore make it our business to learn from the living as well as from the dead.

III. *The gentleman is slow of speech, resolute in action.*[8]

The word I have translated by " gentleman " is *chün-tzŭ*, one of the key-words of Confucianism and one which Dr. Legge rendered, rather ponderously perhaps, by the term " the superior man." My own preference for " gentleman " is, I think, justifiable, and I adopt it with the more confidence because it completely satisfied the fastidious taste of one of the most brilliant of modern Chinese men of letters— Liang Ch'i-ch'ao. In one of his books he declared that " gentleman " was the nearest possible equivalent of *chün-tzŭ*.[9] In making that statement he paid the highest compliment that could possibly be paid by the spirit of Confucian China to the kindred spirit that inspires what has been called the " lay religion " of the English.[10] Another equivalent for *chün-tzŭ*, perhaps equally satisfactory, is to be found in the Aristotelian μεγαλόψυχος—in its good sense.[11]

The *chün-tzŭ*, then, or the gentleman, should be slow of speech, resolute in action. It is the practice of the commoner kind of man, says Chêng Hsiao-hsü, to be readier with words than with deeds. The gentleman, on the other hand, is readier with deeds than with words. The true Confucian is more concerned with right action than with cunning talk. Those who hear and see him may complain of his reticence, but they will never have cause to complain of his failure to act. When he speaks, men trust his words, not because he is a speaker but because they know his words will be more than confirmed by his deeds. Those who are of ready tongue but are slow to act are not followers of the Confucian way. " The words of the *chün-tzǔ*," we read elsewhere, " are few but full of meaning ; the small man's words are many but vain."[12]

These are sentiments which find an echo in many a Western heart to-day. Dr. L. P. Jacks was wearing the mantle of Confucius, though perhaps he knew it not, when he complained, a few years ago, that " men attach greater value to what they *say* . . . than to what they *do*." He expressed his concurrence with St. James and with Thomas Carlyle (he might well have added Confucius) in the view that the " tongue, or speech-making faculty in general, whether acting in the primitive manner or through the printing-press, is a slippery, deceitful and dangerous power which, far from being entitled to govern, stands more in need of being governed than any other power possessed by man." Dr. Jacks is equally Confucian when he denounces the habit of " attaching more importance to what is said by speaking persons than to what is *done* by working persons."[13]

A distinguished French writer of our own time, M. André Maurois, tells us that " only in taking action does the Englishman discover what he wants to do." If this be a true saying, here is fresh evidence that a kinship of spirit exists between the Englishman and the Confucian.[14]

IV.   *Tzŭ-Lu said—" Master, will you tell us what your ambitions are ? " The master replied : " It is my ambition to give rest and peace to the aged, to be loyal and faithful to my friends, to give loving care to the young."*[15]

At first sight these " ambitions " seem to be lacking in comprehensiveness, and hardly worthy of a great world-teacher. Fully to understand the answer given by Confucius to his disciples' question, it would be necessary not only to read the context but also to take into account that fundamental Confucian doctrine which insists that the development of character must begin with self-discipline and self-control in solitude and in the family, that conduct must be based on perfect sincerity and purity of motive, and that moral endeavour must operate in gradually-widening circles.[16] According to well-known passages in the canonical work " The Higher Learning " or *Ta Hsüeh*, and the *Chung Yung*, or " Doctrine of the Mean," in which this teaching occupies a prominent place, a man must be " watchful over himself when he is alone," for the character of his soul is built up in solitude and makes itself outwardly manifest when he moves among men. Conduct which has the external appearance of correctness but is actually founded on base or selfish motives, will sooner or later reveal itself in its true ugliness.[17] The sincerity of a man's actions can be tested by observing how he behaves in his domestic and social relationships. If he is a good son, a trustworthy friend, a devoted father, he may be relied upon to be a loyal subject. If he is entrusted with great reponsibilities, or is called to the highest position in the State, he will be a model ruler and earn the respect and affection of his people. " From the emperor down to the common people," says *The Higher Learning*, " all right conduct must spring from self-discipline. . . . The ruler need not go beyond his own family to prove his worthiness to be the guide and teacher of his people. One family sets an example of the highest virtue, and the whole nation will be virtuous ; one family excels in gracious courtesy and the whole nation will be courteous."

The good man, observes Chêng Hsiao-hsü, does not allow his wider interests to absorb his energies to the neglect of the duties that lie near at hand ; but with utter sincerity and unselfishness and a well-disciplined will, he gives rest and peace to the aged, loving care to the young, and loyalty and good faith to those with whom he is brought into daily contact. He will then have proved his capacity to undertake the greater tasks that lie beyond. Thus he begins with self-discipline, he proceeds to the proper discharge of his duties to his family, and he gradually extends the sphere of his activities to all his relations with his fellow-men. There are no theoretical limits to that extension, and in principle his activities may reach to the limits of his social and political environment and perhaps transcend them.[18]

Taking the text in its most limited sense, we may fittingly compare it with the well-known lines of Robert Burns :

> " *To mak a happy fireside clime*
> *To weans and wife,*
> *That's the true pathos and sublime*
> *Of human life.*"[19]

Had the Scottish poet been versed in Chinese literature he might have been suspected of having read a Chinese poem composed six hundred years or more before the Christian era :

> *Loving communion with wife and children*
> *Is like the music of lutes ;*
> *Happy concord among brethren*
> *Is a melody sweet and lasting.*[20]

V. *Uprightness belongs to man by virtue of his birth ; if he loses that, he is in peril.*[21]

Here we have affirmed a characteristic Confucian doctrine—the natural goodness of man's nature. Its truth was assumed in the comments on the first of our fourteen texts. There was a time when many Christian missionaries in China took this as " a direct contradiction "—to use the words of the Rev. J. Edkins—" of the Christian doctrine of man's original depravity."[22]

Doolittle, another missionary, gave in his book, *The Social Life of the Chinese*, an appalling description of the depth of moral infamy in which he believed the Chinese to be wallowing, and was distressed to observe that these unfortunate creatures would not admit " the reasonableness or the truth of the Bible doctrine of the innate and universal depravity of human nature."[23]

We are now told that the natural vileness of mankind is " emphatically not the teaching of the Christian Church, the orthodox doctrine being that human nature is essentially good, however much it may be buried underneath the rubbish of ignorance and evil."[24] This view is not that of Mr. T. S. Eliot, for whom the doctrine of Original Sin remains " a very real and tremendous thing " ;[25] nor is it easily reconcilable with the statement in the Westminster Confession, that " original sin " is an " original corruption, whereby we are utterly indisposed . . . to all good and wholly inclined to all evil." James Ward, however, declares that it is a " questionable theological dogma that has been discredited,"[26] and A. E. Taylor goes so far as to describe it as " an outrageous unfact," and would welcome " any scientific Theism which would dispense us from the necessity of believing in so ridiculous a slander on human nature."[27]

If it be true that the essential goodness of human nature has now been ascertained to be orthodox Christian teaching, we may find satisfaction in the thought that in this matter, as in many others, Confucianism and Christianity are absolutely at one. They are at one, moreover, with Aristotle and with Plotinus, both of whom assert that " the ' nature ' of everything is the best that it can grow into " ; to which, says Dr. Inge, they would add that " the best of human nature is divine."

The doctrine of the goodness of human nature was affirmed in the fourth century B.C. by Mencius—the " Second Sage " of the Confucian School—even more precisely than by Confucius himself, and it is explicitly stated in the opening words of a famous little book— the San Tzŭ Ching or "Trimetrical Classic"—which till recent years was regularly committed to memory by every little Confucian.[28] Different views have been put forward from time to time in China as elsewhere. The School of Kao Tzŭ, an opponent of Mencius, taught that human nature was neither good nor bad. Hsün Tzŭ (Hsün K'uang), who according to Dr. Hu Shih lived from about 305 to 235 B.C., was the famous exponent of the view that it is radically bad.[29] The school of Shih Shuo, which included Ch'i-tiao Kai, Kung-sun Ni Tzŭ and others, held that human nature was both good and bad and that the degree of goodness or badness in any adult depended on the success or failure of his education. Early in the Han dynasty, Tung Chung-shu (2nd century B.C.) tried to reconcile the views of Shih Shuo and Hsün Tzŭ. The illustrious Han Yü (768–824) of the T'ang dynasty, divided humanity into three classes : first, the thoroughly good, who could not be made better by education ; second, the thoroughly bad, whom no education could improve ; third, the " mixed," who approximated to the first or to the second class in accordance with the conditions of their education and environment. The Sung philosophers, who wrote voluminously on the subject, mainly agreed with the orthodox view championed by Mencius. Possibly in this they were influenced by Mahāyāna Buddhism, which taught that the *Fo hsing* or " Buddha-nature " is common to all beings, who are therefore fundamentally good, and that *ta ti chung shêng ch'êng Fo*—" all beings in the universe will become Buddha " or will enter into the state of Buddhahood.

Apart from the fact that there is now, apparently, no essential difference of opinion between Confucian and Christian orthodoxy on this question of human nature, it is a subject which in the light of modern scientific knowledge seems hardly worth discussing. The science of psychology had not come into existence in the days of Confucius, and certainly neither he nor his successors had any knowledge of the problems of human character and behaviour which arise out of recent researches into the nature and functions of the human glands. They knew nothing of what has recently beeen called " the imbalance of the endocrines."[30] Nor were they aware of the moral deterioration in the human personality sometimes brought about by certain diseases that affect the stability of the nervous system.

It is in connection with the doctrine of the inherent goodness of human nature, however, that we should seek the meaning of the references in Mencius and other Confucian writers to the *ch'ih-tzŭ hsin*—the " child's heart "—which man should endeavour to maintain in its original purity. Mencius said in a famous passage that the man who is truly great is one who " does not lose his child's heart," which may remind us of Schopenhauer's " every genius is a great child."[31] It may also remind us of another great saying— " except ye be converted and become as little children, ye shall not enter into the kingdom of heaven." In drawing attention to this parallel, Dr. Legge points out that whereas Christ speaks of the child-heart as " a thing to be regained," Mencius speaks of it as " a thing not to be lost." Perhaps rather harshly he stigmatises what he assumes to be Mencius's meaning as " absurd."[32]

However we may choose to interpret this famous saying of Mencius, it is interesting to find modern writers arriving independently at the standpoint of the Chinese sage. Mr. H. Belloc, I think, has said somewhere, " surely the end of any act of religion is to get the heart of a child." John Burroughs was not, perhaps, a religious man in the conventional sense, yet one of his admirers once said of him, " Verily he has what Björnson called ' the child in the heart.' "[33] " Children, and older persons who retain something of the habits of children," says a writer on poets and poetry, " are wisest and best."[34] " C'est l'enfant qui est plein," said Charles Péguy, " et l'homme qui est vide."

I was glad to see the genial Confucian view of human nature endorsed very recently by the vice-chancellor of one of Bristol's sister-universities. Speaking on November 18th, 1933, and referring to his long career

at St. Andrew's, Sir James Irvine used these words :
" Perhaps the thing most prominent in my mind is
this—that my experience has given me still higher
appreciation of the inherent goodness of human
nature."[35]

VI.   *In his teaching, the Master made four subjects his chief
concern—scholarship, right conduct, loyalty to duty, and
sincerity.*[36]

The Chinese characters have a wider meaning than
the corresponding English terms—the first might be
better translated " cultural subjects "—but perhaps
Chêng Hsiao-hsü is not far wrong when he says that
if a student were to absorb all that Confucius meant by
these terms, he would be a *wan jên*—" a complete
man." The Confucian teaching aimed at man's moral
and intellectual development, with emphasis on the
former as the more important of the two. Our English
public-school system is understood to have as its primary
aim the formation of character. The Confucian system
of education is inspired by the same ideal. To quote the
words of Lu Hsiang-shan, *hsüeh chê so i wei hsüeh, hsüeh
wei jên erh i :* " the whole aim of education is simply
this—to learn how to be a man." Intellectual training
was not neglected, but moral discipline was put first.

I will translate two consecutive passages from the
Confucian *Lun Yü* and one from the *Li Chi* to
show how strong was the emphasis laid by the Master
on the necessity of subordinating mere learning to
character.

" The Master said, ' A youth should be filial at home, respectful abroad, earnest and truthful in all his social relations. He should have love for all, but seek the friendship only of the best. Then, with what strength he has to spare, he may study literature and the arts.' "

" Tzŭ-Hsia said, ' If a man do honour to moral excellence and turn away from sensual indulgence ; if to the utmost of his power he serve his father and mother ; if he be ready to give his life for his prince ; if in his friendships his language be ever sincere : though he have no learning, I hesitate not to pronounce him a true scholar.' "

The passage from the *Li Chi* or " Record of Rites and Ceremonial " is as follows :

" The practice of right living is the highest of all arts. Other arts are of minor importance. First to be aimed at is the moral life ; all else is subordinate. This was understood by the ancient royal sages, who knew how to assign all human activities to their proper places, the higher and the lower. It was thus that they were able to provide the whole kingdom with the right music and the right ceremonial."[37]

The significance of the last sentence will be clearer when we come to deal with the subject of Music and Ceremonial in the Confucian system.

Not long ago, the Berlin correspondent of *The Times*, discussing the subject of " Nazi Culture," observed of the new educational ideal in Germany that " the professor will no longer merely impart knowledge ; he must lead and inspire his pupils " ; and that " character and not learning, general culture and not specialised knowledge, will be demanded."[38] Perhaps, after all, there was nothing very novel about this " new educational ideal." It was a Chinese ideal more than two thousand years before it was either German or British. And was it not a Greek ideal too ? The Socrates of the *Memorabilia*, in answer to someone who asked him what should be the principal subject of study, replied " right conduct."

It is necessary to emphasise the Confucian teaching on the supreme importance of the training of character, because during the later periods of Chinese history this teaching tended to be lost sight of, and the famous " examination system," conducted on ultra-conservative lines, in which the spirit of Confucianism was almost wholly lacking, called for strenuous mental efforts to memorise the classics and write essays on the classical model. The system had become ossified, and deserved to be broken up. Devoted followers of Confucius, like K'ang Yu-wei in 1898, were the first to demand its abolition. But it should be needless to say there was no necessary connection between Confucianism and the examination system with its " eight-legged " essays.

Although character and conduct are always given precedence over mere book-learning, the latter is also recommended and cherished. The following anecdote, told by Liu Hsiang, has a bearing on this point.

A Courtyard of the Confucian Temple at Ch'ü-Fou

" Tzŭ-Kung asked Tzŭ-Shih why he was showing slackness in his studies. 'I have no time for them,' replied Tzŭ-Shih. 'My parents exact filial piety from me, my brothers exact fraternal duty, my friends exact good faith. What time have I for anything more than the study of these duties?' 'I suggest,' said Tzŭ-Kung, 'that you come to my Master [Confucius] and let him be your teacher.' "

Tzŭ-Kung meant, of course, that Confucius would be able to show Tzŭ-Shih how he could submit himself to all the discipline that might be necessary for his moral development without neglecting the intellectual side of his nature.[39]

VII. *The wise are not shaken by doubt, nor the good by anxiety, nor the stout-hearted by fear.*[40]

This is merely a way of saying that the wise, the good and the brave are clear-sighted, know what is expected of them, and do not falter in right action. He who is over-sceptical will not attain true wisdom ; he who is always perplexed about how he ought to act, and worried about whether he has acted wrongly, will be paralysed by irresolution ; and he who is unable to keep his fears under control cannot be described as a man of true courage. But proper training and self-discipline help one to overcome these imperfections and disabilities.

Such is the best paraphrase I can offer of Chêng Hsiao-hsü's commentary on this text.

VIII. *Fan Ch'ih asked a question about the way in which
kindly sympathy manifests itself in action. The Master
said : " In the domestic relationships it is shown in the
maintenance of a balance between familiarity and reserve ;
in the management of affairs, it is shown in courtesy ; in
general intercourse with mankind it is shown in loyalty
and good faith. Even when contact is made with uncivilised peoples, kindly sympathy must not be with-
held.*"[41]

The Chinese term I have translated by "kindly
sympathy" is *Jên*, perhaps the most important of all
the Confucian keywords and one for which no adequate
equivalent exists in any European language. Among
the English translations suggested and adopted by
different writers are Love, Benevolence, Sympathy,
Charity, Humanity, Goodness of Heart, the Highest
Virtue, Loving Kindness, Unselfishness, Altruism and
the Feeling of Fellowship. None of these terms, singly
used, is comprehensive enough to bring out all the
meanings of *Jên*. "Love," in the New Testament sense,
is appropriate in many passages, but Mr. Leonard
Lyall, one of the latest of English translators of some
of the Confucian classics, is hardly justified in using
it as frequently as he does. The Chinese themselves
have discussed the meaning of *jên* in innumerable
treatises and they find it inexhaustible.[42]

One of the most readily-accepted significations of the
word is that of active sympathy with one's fellow-men.
A famous and oft-quoted remark of Confucius is *ssŭ
hai chih nei chieh hsiung-ti yeh :* " within the four seas "

—supposed to be the boundaries of the known world—
" all are brothers."[43] Thus there is nothing strange to
the Confucian mind in the closing sentence of the text
quoted, which includes " barbarians " or " uncivilised
peoples " among those to whom *jên*—here to be taken
as meaning love or kindly sympathy—is to be extended.

In view of these and many similar utterances in the
Chinese classics it is astonishing to find a distinguished
English visitor to China declaring that " no Confucian
recognises the universal brotherhood of man ; that is
solely a Christian doctrine."[44]

Much fairer and more generous is the tribute paid to
Confucianism by one who cannot be regarded as a
blind admirer of Oriental thought. Alexander Suther-
land observes that " the earliest dawn of a sympathy
that should be both warm and wise is undoubtedly to
be traced among the Chinese," with whom " benevolence is not to consist in the mere giving of alms, it is
to show itself by a willing sympathy towards all men. . . .
The Chinese vindicated in ages now long past their
claim to be the first of truly benevolent peoples."[45]

A contemporary Chinese writer on Confucianism—
Hsieh Tsu-hsien—argues in eloquent language that
the two words which together contain the essence of
Confucianism as a world-saving (*chiu shih*) doctrine are
jên—love, benevolence, humanity—and *chih*—wisdom.
He illustrates this by a well-known passage in the book
of *Mencius*, which I translate as follows :

" Tzŭ-Kung addressing Confucius said, ' Master,
are you a Sage ? ' Confucius replied : ' Nay, that I
Cc

cannot say. I am never weary of learning, I am always ready to teach—that much I can say of myself.' 'Master,' replied Tzŭ-Kung, 'you are never weary of learning—that shows how wise you are ; you are always ready to teach—that shows how loving you are. Endowed as you are with Love and Wisdom— Master, in very truth you are a Sage.' "[46]

Hsieh Tsu-hsien concludes a thoughtful discussion of this subject by pointing out that Love is the essence or the " deep heart " (*shên hsin*) of the Confucian doctrine of salvation ; but that Love without Wisdom is incapable of transmuting itself into right action, while Wisdom without Love is a sterile or a dangerous thing.

IX. *Tzŭ-Kung asked if the Master could give him one word to serve as a rule of life. The Master said : " Would not ' Reciprocity' be such a word ? What you do not wish others to do to you, do not do unto others."*[47]

Dr. Legge, in a note on this well-known text, suggests that an alternative to " reciprocity " as a translation of the Chinese *shu* would be " altruism."[48] Dr. Lionel Giles prefers " charity," for the reason, as he says, that " it really stands for something higher than the strictly utilitarian principle of *do ut des*." He adds that " both here and in another famous passage it is almost equivalent to *jên*, goodness of heart, only with the idea of altruism more explicitly brought out."[49]

This Confucian text has perhaps attracted more attention from Western students than any other saying of Confucius, though it is only one of several passages in the canon in which the Golden Rule, in one form or another, is enunciated.[50] It is sometimes urged that the rule is less striking in its negative than in its positive and Christian form ; but as several writers, including Dr. H. A. Giles, have pointed out, the negative injunction, if faithfully carried out, would have the same practical effect as the positive, and is in principle identical with it.[51] Similarly, J. M. Robertson says that " rationally constructed for ordinary life, the ' do not ' is equivalent to the ' do,' as it bars negative no less than positive forms of unsociability."[52] It was a common practice of the Chinese philosophers to express affirmations in a negative form, and it is often merely a matter of literary style.[53] Moreover, Dr. Legge himself admits that in the *Chung Yung* (" Doctrine of the Mean ") we have the rule " virtually in its positive form." Here, he adds, Confucius " recognises the duty of taking the initiative,—of behaving himself to others in the first instance as he would that they should behave to him."[54]

Mr. Bernard Shaw has informed us that the only Golden Rule is that there are no golden rules ; on which Mr. G. K. Chesterton has made the apt comment that Mr. Shaw prefers an Iron Rule—as in Russia.[55] It is encouraging to note that, in spite of Mr. Shaw, there is one country in the world in which the Golden Rule has almost, if not quite, embodied itself in the whole nation. We were informed not long ago—by an American writer—that " the United States is the nearest thing to the Golden Rule that has yet appeared in nations."[56]

Most people will agree that even if no nation has yet achieved the distinction of being a visible embodiment of it, the Golden Rule, if it is to deserve its name, should be applied to nations and races as well as to individuals, and it is highly creditable to Confucius that, as we have already seen, he included " barbarians " or uncivilised peoples among those to whom *jên*, kindly sympathy or love, was to be extended.[57] It should be added that the Chinese philosopher Mo Ti (probably fourth century B.C.) applied the principle of the Golden Rule in the most emphatic way not only to individuals but also to states. He preached universal love between man and man, neighbour and neighbour, prince and minister, state and state. Whence it follows that although he was himself a great military expert (his special talents lying in the defence of cities) he denounced war in vehement terms.[58] Mo Ti was a *bête noire* to Mencius, for reasons some of which may have been valid ; but in recent years he has come to be recognised as one of the greatest and most original thinkers China has ever produced, and if Confucianism is ever to recover its lost predominance among the Chinese people, there is no doubt that it must withdraw the stigma of heresy which has always attached to Mo Ti as a result of the disapproval of Mencius. Mo Ti, I suggest, should be baptised, however belatedly, into the Confucianism of to-day, in spite of his rejection as a heretic by the Confucianism of yesterday. He would not be the first of the world's great heretics to be acclaimed as a champion of orthodoxy.[59]

X. *The commander of a mighty army may be carried off to captivity, but the humblest man of the people has a will which need never be surrendered.*[60]

In this text, which reminds us of a doctrine of Epictetus, we have another clear and vivid enunciation of the principle of the essential dignity of human nature. Rank and power may be lost, and the body may be deprived of liberty, but the human spirit cannot—unless it consents to its own undoing—be overcome. If the will be directed towards the accumulation of material wealth and honours, the result may be emptiness, desolation, and moral enslavement ; but if it be directed towards the riches that are incorruptible, it will never suffer loss and will never sacrifice its freedom.

XI. *The true scholar and the man of true virtue will never seek to save themselves at the cost of their moral integrity. In its defence they will be ready to sacrifice life itself.*[61]

That the " scholar " should receive the same praise that is accorded to the good man is typical of Confucian thought. The " scholar " is not worthy of the name if his intellectual attainments are not rooted in character. The good man is not necessarily a scholar, but the scholar, if he is not a sham one, must be a good man. Character and learning should go hand in hand, but as we have seen in connection with the sixth of our texts, the greater of these is character.

This text may perhaps be said to be a Confucian version of the great saying, " Whosoever will save his life shall lose it and whosoever will lose his life shall find it," which, according to A. E. Housman, " is the most important truth which has ever been uttered, and the greatest discovery ever made in the moral world.[62] Housman also quotes Blake :

> 'Tis man's perdition to be safe
> When for the truth he ought to die.

XII. *The gentleman (chün-tzŭ) contemplating the world, is free from unreasonable likes and dislikes. He stands for what is right.*[63]

This is a saying which the party-politician—and not he alone—would do well to bear in mind. Neither the Chinese nor the people of any other race are exempt from liability to be swayed by prejudice and passion but the dignity and poise and quiet reasonableness which, till recently at least, were marked characteristics of the educated classes in China, were no doubt in large measure due to their Confucian training.

XIII. *If Truth has been revealed to you in the morning, you may die when night comes without repining.*[64]

In his comment on this text, Chêng Hsiao-hsü refers again to the heaven and hell theories of *wai chiao* (" foreign religions ") which, he says, are superstitions that mislead the foolish. Believers in these *wai chiao* have hopes and fears of what comes after death ; but the life and conduct of the true Confucian are not influenced by such hopes and fears. He knows that he must die, and he shares with the rest of the human race a natural dread of death ; but having been a seeker after truth during his lifetime he accepts death, when it comes, with equanimity, knowing not only that it is the common lot of all but that he has experienced life to the full, in depth if not in length of years. Why should he yearn to prolong life, seeing that all that was worth doing has been done?

XIV. *Among the truly educated, there is no distinction of classes.*[65]

The sentence which I so translate consists of four Chinese characters—*yu chiao wu lei*. This extreme conciseness, as is so often the case with classical Chinese, makes translation difficult and opens the way to various interpretations. Ku Hung-ming, a Chinese who was educated in Great Britain and produced an English translation of the Confucian *Lun Yü* which has many merits in spite of its diffuseness, translates the sentence thus : " Among really educated, civilised people there is no Nationalism or race distinction."[66] This translation was published by him in a Peking newspaper in 1923, and it differs slightly from his original version, which was as follows : " Among really educated men, there is no caste or race-distinction."[67] The difference between the two translations (the first published in 1898, the second a quarter of a century later), illustrates the manner in which Confucian texts lend themselves to reinterpretation ; or perhaps we should say, how Confucian writers may adapt a classical text to new conditions which were unknown in Confucius's time and extract from them lessons for a later age.

Caste, though not a Chinese institution even in the time of Confucius, had a meaning for Ku Hung-ming, so he had no hesitation in introducing the idea into his translation of this text in 1898. Twenty-five years later he had ceased to be interested in caste, but the Great War had caused him to think a good deal about Nationalism and its perils, and he had also pondered on the subject of true and false " civilisations." So he introduced both these ideas into his translation of 1923. It is safe to say that Confucius, when he uttered the words which are crystallised in this text, was not thinking about either caste or nationalism.[68]

We observe from this example that the conciseness of Chinese classical phraseology has its dangers ; nevertheless it cannot be denied that just as a Christian teacher may feel justified in using Biblical texts to reinforce teachings of which the original writer of those texts was ignorant, or in reinterpreting them so as to make them applicable to a social or political environment of which the Biblical writers had no conception, so a Confucian writer may make similar use of Confucian texts, and indeed must do so if Confucianism is to be treated as a living and not as a dead system.

Legge translates the passage more simply, although —in spite of his reliance on Chinese commentators— I question the accuracy of his interpretation. " In teaching, there should be no distinction of classes."[69] Leonard Lyall's version—" all educated men are peers "—has at least the rare merit of being almost as concise as the Chinese original.[70]

The interpretation of Chu Hsi, the great Sung dynasty philosopher (1130–1200) may be stated as follows. Accepting the orthodox Confucian teaching of the goodness of human nature, he says that men grow up good and bad, and with varying degrees of goodness and badness, because of the influence of upbringing, associations and environment. Thus we have various " classes " (*lei*) of men, not in the social but in the moral and intellectual sense. Now " education " in the widest sense of the word can prevent these " classes " from coming into existence, because a sound educator will lead his pupils in the right way and cause them to grow and develop along the lines of their original nature, which is good. All those, therefore, who receive the right kind of education are in principle potentially equal. If they vary among themselves owing to different mental endowments or other unavoidable causes, they will not fall into different classes. Hence among truly educated men, *lei* or classes do not exist. In other words, education can preserve the original goodness of man's nature, or, if that has already become tainted or grown " crooked," it may by education be restored to its original goodness or straightness.

If Bristol or any other University is in search of a Chinese motto expressive of at least one of its educational ideals, I can suggest none more appropriate than this saying from the Confucian canon—*Yu Chiao Wu Lei*—" Among the truly educated, there is no distinction of classes."[71]

CHAPTER III

FILIAL PIETY

WE HAVE NOW discussed the fourteen texts which were considered by a distinguished Chinese scholar twenty-five years ago to provide sound Confucian material for the education of Chinese boys. He might have chosen a multitude of other texts, many of them perhaps just as useful and characteristic as those selected, but it is evident that he regarded these as adequate for the purpose which he and his fellow-countrymen in Java had in view. I have already observed that much is omitted that a European would have included ; and indeed the texts as they stand are quite inadequate to provide a non-Confucian with a clear answer to the question " What is Confucianism ? " This is due to the fact that Chêng Hsiao-hsü's booklet was intended for Chinese, not for European guidance, and therefore leaves out of account a great deal that is essential to the Confucian system but was so familiar to Chinese teachers and pupils—even in Java—as to need no emphasis. Hence the omission of specific references to such important subjects as filial piety, the keystone of the Chinese ethical arch ; the cult of ancestors ; the " five relationships " which figure so prominently in the canon and later Confucian literature ; the social

and economic doctrines of the Confucian School ; the
political ideals of Confucius ; and last but not least,
his attitude towards the unseen world.

It is obviously impossible for me to deal adequately
with these topics, or to supply the deficiencies of the
fourteen texts of Chêng Hsiao-hsü, in the limited time
at my disposal and yours. A brief indication of the
Confucian approach to some of these important subjects is all that can be attempted.

As to Filial Piety, it has a very much wider significance in Chinese ethics than it has with us. It may be
held to include most of the virtues with which human
nature is or can be endowed, for the simple reason that,
according to Confucian ideas, the man who fails to
carry out his obligations as a son, a husband, a father,
and a member of society, thereby dishonours his
parents and has thus committed a breach of *Hsiao*—
the Chinese term which for want of a better phrase we
render by Filial Piety.[1] A son is unfilial if through vice,
neglect, or other avoidable cause he falls into ill-health
or meets with bodily disaster ; because his body, having
been received from his parents, must, out of respect for
them, be treated with scrupulous care. He is unfilial
if he commits a crime, because, by rendering himself
liable to legal penalty, he has brought disgrace upon
his parents. There is indeed very little in the way of
moral achievement or failure that cannot in Chinese
eyes be estimated in terms of the degree of its conformity with or departure from the all-embracing virtue
of *Hsiao*.[2]

According to a passage in the *Lun Yü*, the Master

said, " filial piety is shown by children when nothing but unavoidable illness makes them a source of anxiety to their parents."[3] This may remind us of Boethius, who said, " parents have been tortured by their children "—meaning " by anxiety on their account." But Boethius, unlike Confucius, meant his words to be a consolation to the childless, and it is with approval that he quotes Euripides, who declared that those who have no children are happy in their misfortune.[4]

The loyalty that a man owes to his country or to his sovereign is commonly known by the specific term *chung*, but Chinese moralists have included this virtue also under the head of Filial Piety, on the ground that the emperor was Father of his people and therefore commanded their filial obedience.[5]

The emperor himself was expected to set an example of filial piety to the whole empire. We are told that " the way " of the model rulers of remote antiquity, Yao and Shun, was " filial piety and fraternal affection —these and nothing else " (*Yao Shun chih tao Hsiao T'i erh i i*).[6] By this we are to understand that Hsiao, in its widest signification, included all the virtues proper to a royal sage. This being so, Confucian propriety demanded that every sovereign should, as far as in him lay, imitate those infallible predecessors of his who lived (or did not live) in the third millennium B.C. I have shown elsewhere that this principle might and sometimes did have highly inconvenient and even dangerous results for the Throne and for the State.[7]

It is not surprising that in this revolutionary age the doctrine of filial piety has been fiercely assailed not only by those who object to the traditional association between filial piety and loyalty to a sovereign but also by those who are restive under the restraints and obligations of the Chinese family system. Dr. Hu Shih, well known for his participation in various reform movements, is one of many writers of the new school who have denied the right of filial piety to the place of honour among the virtues. Dr. Hu, in fact, appears to regard it as no virtue at all. One of his letters on this subject has been included in an anthology of essays by various hands primarily intended for the use of schools, and there is no doubt that it has met with a sympathetic reception from thousands of Chinese schoolboys and university students who have found the burden of family-obligations too irksome to be borne. In that essay he absolves his own son from all " filial " duty, and assumes towards him an attitude which is almost apologetic. " Certainly," he says in effect, " my son owes me no gratitude for having caused him to be brought into the world, and I neither wish nor hope for any return or acknowledgment from him. If when he grows up he chooses to show gratitude for what I may have done for him, that is his own affair. Unquestionably I cannot claim gratitude from him as a right."[8]

The decay of " filial piety " in the New China is all the more significant when we remember how recently it was that the Chinese held Western civilisation in low esteem largely because they thought it failed to give adequate recognition to that virtue. Many *mo-têng* Chinese (*mo-têng* is a new and very popular phrase which represents the English " modern ") might be surprised and perplexed to learn that in a college for women in Boston, U.S.A., a vote was recently taken on the question of the relative importance and value of the Ten Commandments, and that by a large majority the Fifth Commandment was placed first.[9]

Dr. Legge, in a footnote to his edition of Mencius, quotes the following words from one of Charles Lamb's letters to Coleridge. " Oh, my friend, cultivate the filial feelings ; and let no one think himself relieved from the kind charities of relationship : these shall give him peace at the last ; these are the best foundation for every species of benevolence."[10] These words might have been written by a Confucian sage instead of by an English " saint."

CHAPTER IV

TEACHER AND PUPIL

If the relationship between child and parent and the obligations attaching to it occupy the central position in the Chinese ethical system, scarcely less important is the stress laid on the relationship between teacher and pupil. It is not enumerated among the *Wu Lun*—" the Five Human Relationships "—but it has a close affinity to two of them, those of parent and child and friend with friend. A Chinese scholar of to-day, whom I have already quoted, rightly observes that " in China friendship is everything and counts for far more than in any other country. . . . The Chinese social code is the family code writ large, with an ampler place given to the fifth relationship—that of friend to friend. And of friendships, that of the teacher and pupil is considered as the most intimate and weighty ; and this has produced much of Chinese history and a goodly portion of her civilisation."[1]

The Chinese code requires a student to pay the same or very similar respect to his teacher that he would to his father, on the principle that just as a child owes his body to his parents, so he owes his intellectual equipment to his teacher. Physically, he is the offspring of his father and mother ; intellectually, and to a large extent morally, he is the offspring of his teacher.

The *Kuo Yü*—a well-known compilation of the Confucian School—declares that there are three persons who should be looked up to by each individual with equal devotion : his father, who gives life ; his teacher, who shows how life is to be lived ; and his prince, who provides the conditions of a good life by maintaining the social order.[2]

Dr. W. A. P. Martin—for many years himself engaged in educational work among the Chinese—rightly observes that in no country was the office of teacher more revered than it was in China. " Not only is the living instructor saluted with forms of profoundest respect, but the very name of teacher, taken in the abstract, is an object of almost idolatrous language."[3]

In the schools of Old China—by which I mean prerevolutionary China—the pupils did homage first to " the most holy Sage K'ung Fu Tzŭ "—whose spirit-tablet was there to remind them that Confucius was the wisest of teachers and the father of Chinese civilisation—then to their schoolmaster, who was the Sage's living representative.

So honourable was the position of a teacher in China that even the Emperor was obliged to show deference to his tutor, not only before but after he had ceased to be *in statu pupillari*. " The Son of Heaven," as a recent Chinese commentator on the *Li Chi* points out, " occupied the most exalted position in the State, yet the ancient books declare that there was one to whom even the Son of Heaven had to yield precedence—namely, his teacher. Therefore according to the old Chinese system, no title was more exalted than that of imperial tutor, for he owed no obedience to anyone in the land, however rich or noble or influential." An imperial tutor, as I have explained elsewhere, was the only person who did not face the north when admitted to the Emperor's presence : the reason being that the relationship between them was not that of subject and ruler.[4]

The Confucian theory of the place of education in the life of the individual and of the community is in full harmony with that which is slowly emerging out of the political and social chaos of our own day. " Since education," says Mr. W. Olaf Stapledon, " is of all the community's services the most important and the most highly skilled, teaching should be the most honoured of all professions. . . . Care should be taken that the profession actually deserves to be honoured. Only persons of high mental calibre should be allowed to teach, and only those who have also the special ability of the teacher."[5]

It is true that the Confucian School did not contemplate a state of society in which it would be possible that all the healthy members of a State should not merely be educated but have access to equal educational advantages. Being unaware of the coming of an age when machinery would displace unskilled labour and routine skill, and when " education for leisure " would become a pressing social necessity, Confucianism assumed that human society consisted and must always consist of two great classes—the brain-workers and the hand-workers—and that the latter must necessarily be engaged in ceaseless manual toil and accept the guidance of the former. Confucius cannot be blamed for this assumption, which was a natural and inevitable

Dc

one not only in his day but almost down to our own. "Before the days of mechanical power," as Mr. Stapledon says, " society depended almost entirely on human muscles ; and so much muscular work had to be done that most individuals in a society could not possibly have either opportunity or desire for education."[6]

If we compare the China of to-day with the China of thirty or forty years ago, we shall find nothing more startling and even alarming than the change that seems to have come over the relationship between teacher and pupil. At first sight, at least, it would appear that the traditional reverence of pupil for teacher—though it was maintained in the imperial palace as long as the Court existed—has wholly disappeared. In some schools and colleges the relative positions of teacher and taught seems to have been reversed. It is apparently no longer the student's duty to obey his teacher ; it is rather the teacher's duty to walk humbly and circumspectly in the path pointed out to him by the student. There are schools in which the students have not only driven the teaching staff from their posts but have claimed the right to nominate the successors of those whom they have expelled. There are Government universities in which the students have refused to recognise the person nominated by the Board of Education to fill the post of president. Many college principals and professors have been insulted and beaten, and terrorised into flight or resignation. A few years ago the newspapers reported a case of the head of a college in Western China who, after being brutally assaulted by his students, was thrown into a well and left to drown. In certain colleges the students, having failed to pass their examinations, or being too much engrossed in politics to attend to such trivial affairs as lectures and qualifying classes, have declared the abolition of the examination-system. School-strikes (*pa k'o*) have become so common as to arouse no public comment, and student-tumults (*hsüeh-ch'ao*) are reported almost weekly from every province.

Ever since the beginning of the famous " student-movement " which by common consent is assigned to May 4th, 1919, the schools and colleges of China have been the breeding-ground of every revolutionary " ism," social, educational and political ; bands of students—very often at the instigation of wire-pullers of whose identity they are ignorant and who keep themselves carefully in the background—have frequently left their class-rooms to march through the streets chanting slogans against foreign " imperialists," " capitalists," national " traitors " or " unequal treaties." They have broken into Government buildings, smashed the furniture, used the legs of tables to assault high officials, drawn blood and tears from cabinet-ministers, and compelled their buffeted victims to undergo the humiliation of accepting foreign protection on Chinese soil.

The political activities of the students, which have often been inspired by patriotic motives, do not concern us here except in so far as they affect the relations between themselves and their teachers. Unfortunately they frequently do affect those relations, because the numerous political and military factions which have for years been struggling with one another for supremacy in China are all anxious to make use of the schools and colleges for political ends. It thus happens that presidents and professors are often the nominees of powerful political parties or individuals and have received their appointments for qualifications which have very little to do with education. Such persons are primarily political propagandists, or the obedient tools of their patrons, or have obtained their posts as a reward for political services. If, as frequently happens, their propaganda meets with a hostile reception from a considerable section of their students, or if the students discover—as they often do—that those who have been placed in authority over them lack the experience and other qualifications that teachers should possess, there is sure to be a *hsüeh-ch'ao*—an outbreak of violent disorder.

Thus when we contemplate the chaotic condition of education in the China of to-day and the apparent break-down of the old system whereby every schoolboy was expected not only to revere his teacher but also to " receive with confidence, meekly and humbly, every word spoken " by him, we must not assume too hastily that this unhappy state of affairs signifies the complete rupture of the traditional relationship between teachers and taught.[7] The blame, in most cases, rests mainly with the teachers or with the cynical politicians who control them.

It is necessary to emphasise the all-important fact that the " human relationships " which occupy so prominent a place in Confucian teaching involve reciprocal obligations. The son owes filial piety to his father, and the spiritual son or pupil owes respect and obedience to his spiritual father or teacher ; but the father's duties to his son do not cease with mere fatherhood, and the teacher's claim to the homage of his pupil lapses if he fails to justify it. It was the teacher's duty, as I have recently pointed out elsewhere, to perform his functions in such a way that his pupil would grow up to be a Confucian gentleman or *chün-tzŭ*— " which meant that he would be a ripe scholar, honourable, modest, sincere, trustworthy in all his dealings and magnanimous to friend and foe." The teacher who failed in his high function " was no more worthy of respect than was a ruler who misgoverned his country." The Roman maxim, *maxima debetur puero reverentia* was enunciated almost in the same words by Confucian teachers long before it was uttered by Juvenal.

Thus if the old relationship of *mutual* respect and reverence between master and pupil in China seems to be dissolving, we should be wrong to seek the sole explanation of this in the rebellious spirit that animates Young China in this iconoclastic age, or even in the decay of the Confucian tradition in every sphere of China's social life. The Chinese students, of whom so many harsh things have been said during the past twenty years, did not originate the chaos we see in the Chinese educational world to-day ; nor do they compel us to abandon, as utterly disproved, the Confucian doctrine of the essential goodness of human nature.

CHAPTER V

THE CULT OF ANCESTORS

VERY CLOSELY ASSOCIATED with *Hsiao* or Filial
Piety is the Cult of Ancestors. It has often been said
that the so-called " worship " of ancestors—" worship "
is far too strong a word—is the real religion of the
Chinese people. What is not sufficiently understood
by those whose knowledge is derived from books or
hostile critics rather than from personal observation
and sympathetic insight is that " ancestor-worship "
has a practical and utilitarian as well as a religious or
spiritual aspect, and is consciously and deliberately
maintained as a method whereby a Chinese family not
only shows its reverence or respect for its departed
forefathers but also maintains the continuity of its
traditions, strengthens its ties with its scattered members and collateral branches, and safeguards the
material interests of its descendants. In actual practice
the cult is not so much a cult of ancestors as a cult of
the family. " Family-worship " would be at least as
good a name for it as " ancestor-worship " and would
give a better indication of its true purport. The cult
of ancestors is indeed only a subdivision, though an
important one, of the cult of the family.

Liang Ch'i-ch'ao, the famous pupil of K'ang Yu-wei,

was well aware of what the cult of ancestors really
meant to his fellow-countrymen, and this is how he
describes it.

    " The family group," he says, in a book which has
recently been translated into English, " underlies the
whole fabric of society. Each smaller group is
gathered up into a larger group, so that all trace
their relationship to the prime ancestor. . . . Therefore it is said in the *Tso Chuan* : ' The way of men is
to love one's relatives. *Because of love for relatives, the
ancestors are honoured ; honour for ancestors brings respect
for the distant relatives ; respect for distant relatives brings
a sense of kinship.*' This family concept constitutes the
fundamental basis of political organisation. *When
this conception is further strengthened by religious ideals, its
effect is the more vigorous.* . . . The logical result of such
concepts is the recognition that all mankind is but
one large family."[1]

    Students of religious beliefs cannot fail to be struck,
when they come to China, by the obvious similarity
between the cult of ancestors, as it exists to-day in that
country, and the similar domestic cults of ancient
Greece and Rome. Warde Fowler points out that in
Rome these cults provided an antidote against a
" degraded polytheism." He refers to the regularity and
simplicity of the ritual, and he adds that it " indicated
a reliance of the family, for its support and continuance,
on certain manifestations of a Power beyond human
control, approachable by all members of the household,

and without a priestly medium to petrify it, as the Graeco-Roman gods had been petrified."[2]

It is " ancestor-worship," we may surmise, which has been mainly instrumental in saving the Chinese people from the evils of priestcraft. The rites of the cult are performed not by priests but by the heads of families or even by the individual members of families. They take place either in the seclusion of the domestic circle or in ancestral temples which are the private property of the families or clans immediately concerned.

The cult of ancestors has been denounced by some foreigners as idolatry, and by others as inimical to the progress of the race because it has taught the Chinese to look back to a vanished past. It would be profitless to revive a dead controversy—very much alive though it was among Catholic missionaries in the seventeenth and eighteenth centuries—by discussing the charge of idolatry. The other charge is perhaps not so easy to refute, yet I believe it to have very little justification. More accurately, I think, we ought to describe " ancestor-worship " as a cult which teaches the Chinese to maintain intact the spiritual and material heritage which is theirs in trust for their own descendants.

If we assume, as I believe we may, that in practice if not in theory the Chinese cult of ancestors is maintained for the benefit of the living members of the family and its descendants, we need not be surprised to learn that it implies no very definite beliefs regarding the unseen world.

Numerous Chinese writers in ancient and modern times have debated the question of the human survival of bodily death, and there has been no attempt on the part of orthodox Confucianism to suppress freedom of thought and discussion on this or allied topics. There is ample evidence that the problem was one which interested the disciples of Confucius ; but no recorded utterance of the Master has been taken as justifying the formulation of a definite solution. One free-thinking speculator of the sixth century of our era—Fan Chên— wrote an essay on " the Annihilation of the Spirit," in which he declared that spirit is to the body what its edge is to the knife. If there be no edge there is nothing that can properly be called a knife ; take away the knife and there will be no edge. The spirit cannot survive the disappearance of the body any more than a knife can continue to exist as such after the disappearance of its edge.

Had Fan Chên lived thirteen centuries later, his opponents might have tried to counter his argument by a reference to the Wonderland Cat, the grin of which survived its bodily disappearance. As it was, his reasoning has never met with a refutation which to the Chinese mind has seemed conclusive, and it has reappeared in various forms in the writings of his materialistic successors. Those Chinese philosophers who disagree with his views are many, but it is a significant fact that the theoretical basis of the cult of ancestors, with its assumption of the continued existence of ancestral spirits, is seldom or never mentioned as providing a final answer to the question of the bodiless survival of the human soul.

The idea underlying the cult of ancestors is not merely

that the dead ancestor is still alive in another sphere (this is disputed by many ancestor " worshippers ") but that he is the personification of the family, which, being a corporation, never dies. Thus it is not the ancestor, but the family, that is deathless. This, or something like it, is the theory that makes the problem of individual immortality seem, to the Chinese mind, irrelevant, and why Chinese who are sceptical about the existence of a life beyond the grave are still able to take a perfectly sincere part in the cult of ancestors.[3]

On the other hand, multitudes of Chinese vaguely " believe in the communion between the living and the dead ; in the power of the living to help the departed . . . and in the power of departed heroes, whose heaven lies in extended ability, to help those who remain within the limitations of this world." If such beliefs are to be denounced as superstitious, the stigma attaches to Christians as well as to Chinese, for the words I have just quoted are not a statement of Chinese notions regarding the dead, but an expression of the beliefs shared with his fellow-Christians by a clergyman of the Church of England.[4]

Even if the Chinese practices relating to the ancestral cult are not wholly free from more or less childish superstitions, it may at least be said that the ceremonial observances which accompany the solemn invocations of their ancestors are harmless in effect and certainly show a greater dignity and decorum, and a tenderer respect for the dead, than we find associated in the West with the once-fashionable pursuits of table-turning and spirit-rapping and with spiritualistic

Carved Marble Pillars and Balustrades in front of the Great Hall (*Ta Ch'êng T'ien*) of the Confucian Temple at Ch'ü-Fou

séances. Whether an oblong wooden tablet bearing the honoured name of a father or ancestor is likely to be more effective than a tea-table or a heart-shaped board, or a professional medium, in attracting the spirits of the departed, may be open to dispute ; but it is not easy to see why it is desirable that the tablet should be thrown ignominiously down from its niche in a humble Chinese cottage or in the family shrine of a clan, or burned as a symbol of " idolatry," while ouija or planchette may, without offence, maintain its honourable position in a London drawing-room.[5]

Thus there is no solid ground for the assertion, often made in the past, that the Chinese turn their ancestors into " gods." It is freely acknowledged by those of the Chinese who have any serious belief in a life beyond the grave that ancestral spirits are obliged to confine their activities to the sphere of their own families, and that even within that narrow sphere their powers are severely circumscribed. Any Chinese will admit with the utmost cheerfulness that his dead father, before whose spirit-tablet (shên-chu) he prostrates himself (just as he used to prostrate himself on ceremonial occasions before his living father) occupies among the innumerable hosts of spirits a position of no greater dignity and influence than he occupied among his friends and neighbours on earth. Ancestral spirits differ from living men mainly in this, that having " shuffled off this mortal coil," they are necessarily liberated from physical disabilities and are free to exercise the functions and capacities (whatever they may be) which are inherent in those who have reached the spiritual plane of existence. During their life on earth they were entitled, according to Chinese ethical principles, to claim the respect and obedience of their sons and grandsons. On the assumption that death does not lead to extinction but is the gateway to spiritual life, Chinese believers hold that true filial piety, which like love and friendship is itself a spiritual thing, is privileged to transcend physical and temporal conditions. They believe that the respect and affection due to father and mother during their earthly life acquire a deeper beauty and solemnity in consequence of the change brought about by death and are converted into a synthesis of elevated emotions to which (if we choose) we need not shrink from giving the name of religious reverence.

> " *Rejoice, ye dead, where'er your spirits dwell,*
> *Rejoice that yet on earth your fame is bright;*
> *And that your names, remember'd day and night,*
> *Live on the lips of those that love you well . . .*
> *Now ye are starry names, above the storm*
> *And war of time and nature's endless wrong*
> *Ye flit, in pictured truth and peaceful form,*
> *Wing'd with bright music and melodious song,—*
> *The flaming flowers of heaven, making May-dance*
> *In dear Imagination's rich pleasance.*"

These are not the utterances of a Chinese " ancestor-worshipper "—they are the words of an English poet-laureate. But may not the Chinese be allowed to give expression to thoughts of a similar kind, and to do so in their own way and in accordance with their own ancestral traditions, even if their way and their traditions seem to those of an alien race and an alien culture to be tainted with foolishness ?

The real and serious objection to the cult of the family and its ancestors is that it has hitherto tended (and, so its hostile critics say, must always tend) to make the family absorb much of the loyalty and devotion that should be given to larger groups, social and national. The Chinese have often been criticised, not unjustly, for their lack of public spirit. Liang Ch'i-ch'ao, with whom I discussed this matter on more than one occasion during his last years, wrote with much warmth on this failing of his countrymen. It is a significant fact that the decay of the family-system, which in relatively small but very influential sections of the Chinese population has already made considerable headway, is being accompanied by a steady growth of nationalism and an increasing interest in public affairs. In other words, much of the old devotion to the family is being directed to the State, and the Chinese for the first time are acquiring a strong consciousness of themselves as a nation.[6] This may be to the ultimate benefit of China and her people ; but up to the present both movements have suffered from the lack of wise guidance, from the antics of patriotic but easily-beguiled and undisciplined students, from " Red " and " Pink " propaganda, and from the anti-foreign and other extravagances of the Left wing of the Kuomintang—the political party which claims Sun Yat-sen, its " Late Leader," as its patron saint. The too rapid disintegration of the family system is already showing signs of causing something like a breakdown of ethical standards and restraints which it is to be hoped is only temporary ; and the too rapid and unregulated growth of nationalism has already led the country into dangerous courses and involved it in grave losses, territorial and other. It has also produced unpleasant manifestations and ugly incidents which have brought no good to China and have greatly distressed, if they have not alienated, many of her warmest foreign friends and sympathisers.

The Chinese, with their age-long experience, should not need to be reminded of a truth which was well expressed eleven years ago by Dr. J. Wilson Harper. " A long experience proves," he says, " that the family life is invaluable, and that, so far from being inconsistent with individual liberty or antagonistic to society, it more than anything else provides the conditions under which freedom is developed, and the strong foundations of a social state are securely laid." He warns those who " maintain that domestic unity is opposed to social unity " of the fate of Rome. " Rome in her best days," he says, " held the family life sacred ; but when she violated that life, dissolute morals sapped her very foundations, and did far more than the armies of her enemies in causing the fall of the Empire. The teachings of history cannot be safely or wisely neglected. They indubitably prove that the family is essential to the State, and also to the unity of the human race."[7]

Fortunately, the disintegration of the Chinese family has not yet gone very far ; and there is reason for hope that the forces which are working for its destruction are not those which will dominate Chinese life when the present revolutionary fever has subsided. Nevertheless, human experience, ancient and modern, seems to show that the Family, as the social unit, must sooner or later share its place with the Individual. Chinese society, based on the family, may have been too static. What man wants, what his inherited and innate qualities demand, is a dynamic society—one which is homogeneous and yet gives full play to individual initiative.[8]

CHAPTER VI

CONFUCIANISM AND POLITICAL LOYALTY

IT CANNOT WITH FAIRNESS be said that Confucius and his teachings are responsible for the excessive devotion of the Chinese people to the family, and the comparative indifference they have shown in the past to the interests of the nation. It is of course true that Confucius laid great emphasis on filial piety ; but it is no less true that he emphasised the duty of loyalty to the prince. Indeed, at the time of the revolution of 1911 and afterwards, it was actually made a cause of bitter complaint against Confucius that he was no fit teacher for a free democracy, because he had taught the duty of loyalty to monarchs.

But the loyalty to monarchs which the Confucian School enjoined was very far from being an unreasoning loyalty. The duties and obligations of princes and their subjects were reciprocal. A prince who misgoverned his people, or refused to accept good advice, or otherwise misbehaved himself to the detriment of the public interest, was regarded as having forfeited the right to govern—a right which was his in trust for specific purposes only. If he failed to fulfil those purposes, the *T'ien-ming* or " ordinance of

Heaven" was withdrawn from him and bestowed upon a worthier.

The teaching of Mencius—the greatest of the successors of Confucius—was so emphatic and outspoken on this subject that many centuries after his death, the first emperor of the Ming dynasty, who reigned from 1368 to 1398, degraded him from his place of honour in the temple of the Confucian cult on the ground that he had shown disrespect to monarchs and was therefore a teacher of " dangerous thoughts." The emperor's action, however, raised such strenuous opposition in Confucian circles that he had to bow to the storm, and the decree of degradation was speedily revoked.[1]

What the views of Mencius were which the emperor Hung-Wu found so objectionable may be gathered from the following passages which I translate from the Book of *Mencius*, part of the " Bible " of orthodox Confucianism.

(1) " ' Let us suppose,' said Mencius during an interview with king Hsüan, ' that one of your majesty's servants, who is about to start on a journey to Ch'u, entrusts his family to the care of a friend. On his return, he finds that the friend has allowed his family to suffer from hunger and cold. What should he do with such a friend ? '

" ' He should have nothing more to do with him,' said the king.

" ' And suppose,' continued Mencius, ' that your majesty had a minister of justice who was incapable

Ec

of controlling his subordinates. How would you deal with such a one ? '

" ' Dismiss him at once,' replied the king.

" ' And if throughout your realm there is observed a lack of good government,' Mencius went on, ' what is to be done then ? '

" The king looked this way and that and changed the subject." [2]

(2) " King Hsüan put this question to Mencius : ' Is it true that T'ang dethroned king Chieh and that prince Wu promoted an insurrection against king Chou ? '

" ' History assures us,' answered Mencius, ' that it was even so.'

" ' Is it lawful, then,' said the king, ' for a minister to put his sovereign to death ? '

" ' He who acts in defiance of the highest moral ideals,' said Mencius, ' is a rascal. He who outrages every principle of honour is a cad. The man who acts as a rascal and a cad is properly described—whatever his position may be—as a contemptible ruffian. *I have heard about the killing of a ruffian named Chou ; I have not heard about the killing of a king.*' "[3]

(3) " ' The most important constituent of the nation,' said Mencius, ' is the people ; next come the tutelary divinities ; last comes the king.' "[4]

Another of the canonical books of Confucianism, the *Ta Hsüeh*, which I have called the " The Higher Learning," contains the following passage :

" When the prince loves what his people love and hates what his people hate, then he may indeed be hailed as their true father. . . . By winning the people the throne is won ; by losing the people the throne is lost."[5]

Equally striking are these words from the canonical *Shu Ching*—the Historical Classic—words which are put into the mouth of the founder of the Chou dynasty, more than 1000 B.C.

" God sees even as my people see ; God hears even as my people hear."[6]

All these utterances were made in Confucian or pre-Confucian China. They might have been made in sixteenth century England. The following words are those of the late professor A. V. G. Allen :

" The most characteristic feature of the English people . . . in the sixteenth century, is the prevailing sense of the presence of God. . . . The State took on a divine character, the king's will was regarded as divine because it was in harmony with the people's will, and the will of the people was reflecting the will of God."[7]

Confucianism, which has been accused of being a bulwark of absolute monarchy, has always recognised the dangers of irresponsible autocracy and has upheld the right of the people to resist and even, if necessary, to depose and slay a tyrannical sovereign. The obligation of loyalty to the prince, which has excited the contempt and ridicule of so many Chinese republicans, was far from being a one-sided affair. To the true Confucian, a prince who paid no heed to the advice of wise counsellors was unworthy of his people's confidence.

Liu Hsiang, a great writer, editor and literary critic of the first century B.C., likens a prince without good ministers to a heron without wings. Although it may have eyes sharp enough to see a hundred miles, it cannot hope to fly to the place it wants to go to. " To travel by water," Liu Hsiang continues, " one must have a boat ; to travel by land one must have a chariot ; and if a prince wishes to achieve success he must have wise ministers. They are his boat and his chariot, as necessary to him as its wings are to a heron."[8]

The same writer, in another of the two books ascribed to him, tells many stories which were intended to convey wholesome warnings to princes and to illustrate the obligation under which they lay to listen to the advice of worthy counsellors. The following are a few examples :

" When Chuang became king of Ch'u he held no court for three years and issued an edict saying : ' WE detest those ministers who have the audacity to criticise the actions of their princes. The civil and religious affairs of this State are at OUR absolute disposal, and if anyone dares to address remonstrances to US on account of anything WE may do, he will be condemned to death without hope of pardon.'

" On receipt of this edict a certain Su Ts'ung spoke as follows : ' Those who hold high office under the king and enjoy large emoluments granted by him, but refrain, because they fear death, from remonstrating with him when he errs, are not acting as loyal ministers.' He thereupon submitted a memorial protesting against the edict."

It is pleasant to know that Su Ts'ung's courage was rewarded. The king not only spared his life but made him his prime minister.[9]

" Once when the prince of Liang was out hunting he saw a flock of wild geese. He descended from his chariot and drew his bow. Seeing a man walking along the path, the prince ordered him to stop. The man paid no attention, and by walking on he startled the geese and caused them to fly off in the opposite direction. The prince was angry and was about to draw his bow and shoot the man, when his chariot-driver, a man named Kung-sun Hsi, dismounted and grasped the arrow, saying ' Do not shoot.' The enraged prince turned to him and said angrily, ' I see you have more consideration for strangers than for your prince. How is that ? ' Kung-sun Hsi replied : ' Formerly, in the days of duke Ching of Ch'i, there was a great drought which lasted three years.[10] On an oracle being consulted it was announced that it would not rain until a human sacrifice had been offered up. On hearing this, duke Ching stepped down from his hall, bowed low and said : ' The reason why I consulted the oracle and prayed for rain was that I was anxious about the welfare of my people. Now it appears I must offer up a human sacrifice. *I offer myself.*' He had hardly finished speaking when heavy rain began to fall throughout hundreds of square miles of territory. Now what was the reason of that ? It was because the duke loved his people and had found favour in the eyes of God. Now you, my prince, were proposing to kill a man for the sake of some wild geese. Had you done so, I should have said you were no better than a beast of prey.'

" The prince of Liang took the arrow from his bow, mounted his chariot, and went home. Entering his chapel he announced to the spirits of his ancestors that he had this day met with great good fortune. ' Other men,' he said, ' when they go hunting, come home with wild birds and beasts ; I have gone hunting, and have come home with wise counsel.' "[11]

The following story portrays the ready wit and fidelity of a Chinese minister who was sent " to lie abroad for the good of his country."

" When war seemed likely to break out between the States of Ch'in and Ch'u, the king of Ch'in sent an envoy to ascertain the policy of Ch'u. On his arrival, the king of Ch'u sent someone to test him. ' Did you consult the oracle before starting on your journey?' asked the Ch'u man. 'Indeed I did,' replied the envoy. 'With what result?' 'The response was entirely favourable.' 'That is an extraordinary thing,' said the Ch'u man. 'I don't think much of the tortoises of your country. As it happens, my king intends to put you to death and to consecrate a new bell with your blood. Where is the good fortune that your oracle foretold for you?'

"'Ch'in and Ch'u,' said the envoy, 'are on the verge of war, and my king sent me here to find out what preparations you were making. If I am put to death, my king will know, by my failure to return, that Ch'u has hostile intentions, and he will be forewarned and in a position to take countermeasures. That was what I meant when I said that the response of the oracle was favourable. Moreover, if dead men have no consciousness, what good will it do you to consecrate a bell with a dead man's blood? If, on the other hand, dead men retain their consciousness, do you really suppose that by putting me to death you will turn me into the friend of your country and the enemy of my own? What I should do if I found myself conscious after death would be to silence all the bells and drums of Ch'u. But if they are silent, how can they be used to communicate orders to your troops in time of battle? Furthermore, I may remind you that to slay the envoy of a neighbour-State and thereby break off relations with it is in flagrant disregard of international usage.'"[12]

The result of this colloquy was that the king of

Ch'u so much admired the envoy's courage and intelligence that he spared his life.

It was not always the prince who was the pupil and the minister the teacher. Sometimes, as in the following instance, the rôles were reversed.

" A man of the Ch'u State presented himself at court with a gift of fish for the king. ' To-day's catch,' he said, ' has been so good that the market is glutted. Though the fish cannot be sold, it would be a pity to throw them away, so I have come to offer them to his majesty.'

" ' Preposterous,' said the ministers, when they reported the matter to the king. ' It is a contemptible gift. Reject it.'

" ' You don't realise,' said the king, ' what a good fellow that fisherman is. Let me tell you something. We know from experience that when the State granaries are crammed with hoarded grain, there may be starvation among the people. When there are too many women in the royal seraglio, the manhood of the nation may suffer from a dearth of wives. When wealth is piled high in the royal treasury, the country may be enduring the hardships of grinding poverty. Such conditions result from the abandonment of the Princely Way. If in the royal kitchens there are fat fish and in the royal stables there are sleek horses, while the people are emaciated with hunger, that is because the ruler is a prince who is leading his country to ruin. I have known for a long time that my treasury is full, but I have not known how to carry out an equitable distribution of my wealth.

" ' Now the fisherman knew all about that, and he has taught me a lesson. I have learned it, and I know at last what I ought to do.'

" He then despatched messengers into the country to find out who were the poor and needy, the orphaned and widowed, and among them he distributed money taken from the royal treasury. He also sent away the superfluous women from the royal seraglio, so that they might become the wives of those who had none. In .acting thus he gave great joy to the people of Ch'u, and the peoples of neighbouring States voluntarily came under his sway.

" Thus it was that the State of Ch'u came to owe its happiness and prosperity to the act of a fisherman who had presented his prince with the fish that he could not sell. Here we have an example of Love and Wisdom in action."13

One of the sayings current in ancient China concerning the relative positions and duties of princes and ministers is preserved by Liu Hsiang. " To have a good knowledge of men is the proper qualification of the prince ; to have a sound knowledge of affairs is the proper qualification of the minister."14 In other words, the king should be a good judge of men so that he may select ministers who possess wisdom and experience.

Here it may be mentioned that besides impressing upon monarchs the duty of listening to and acting upon the advice of good counsellors, Mencius also taught, in unmistakable terms, the doctrine of the self-determination of peoples. For example, when the State of Ch'i fought and conquered the State of Yen (two ancient realms which roughly corresponded to parts of the modern provinces of Shantung and Hopei), the ruler of Ch'i asked Mencius to advise him on the question of whether he should annex Yen to his own dominions. The answer given by Mencius was quite explicit. " Annex Yen," he said, " if the people of Yen wish to be annexed. If they do not so wish, refrain from annexation."[15]

In spite of the stress laid by Confucius, Mencius, and their successors on the reciprocal nature of the duties and obligations of sovereign and subject, the mere fact that the first of the *Wu Lun* or " Five Relationships " recognised by the Confucian system was that between *chün* and *ch'ên*—prince and minister—has been enough, as I have said, to condemn Confucianism in the eyes of zealous republicans. But to blame Confucius for his recognition of a patent fact is obviously unreasonable and absurd. The Sage was not guilty of the offence (if it is to be regarded as such) of having invented the *chün-ch'ên* relationship ; it was already in existence long before he was born, and he could not have ignored it any more than he could have ignored the existence of the other four existing relationships— father and son, husband and wife, brother and brother, friend and friend—none of which derived its origin from him. Confucius did not say, " Let there be a prince and a minister " ; he merely taught that existing princes owed courtesy and consideration to their ministers and that existing ministers owed loyalty to their princes. The existence of these persons in Confucius's time may have been a deplorable fact, but Confucius was not responsible for it.

The republican substitute for the prince-and-minister relationship is that of minister (or citizen) and State. The loyalty formerly owed by a minister or a subject to his sovereign is easily and naturally converted into the loyalty owed by a minister or a citizen to the State or to the person who, whatever his title may be, is the State's visible representative or embodiment. In his inaugural speech in 1913, when he became president of the new Chinese republic, Yüan Shih-k'ai declared that " the original meaning of *chung* (loyalty) is loyalty to the State and not to an individual "[16] ; and wiser and better men than Yüan have pointed out the same not very recondite truth.

Some Western and Chinese critics have spoken as though the abolition of the prince-and-minister relationship consequent on the change from monarchy to republicanism involves the collapse of the whole Confucian system. One might as well argue that Christianity cannot exist in a republic because Christ advised men to " render unto Caesar the things that are Caesar's."

CHAPTER VII

IS CONFUCIANISM A RELIGION?

THIS QUESTION is repeatedly put to those who are supposed to know something about Confucius and his system, but it is obviously one to which no definite answer can be given until we have agreed on a definition of religion. As I do not myself presume to offer such a definition, no attempt that I can make to answer the question can be other than tentative and inconclusive.

Nevertheless it is at least possible to clear away some common misunderstandings. One of these is the notion that Confucianism must be placed in the category of religions because Confucius is or has been worshipped as a god. No school of Confucian thought has ever regarded Confucius as a god. As we saw when we were considering the first of the fourteen texts selected by Chêng Hsiao-hsü, the status of Confucius is that of a *shêng-jên* or " Sage." We are repeatedly told that the Sage belongs to the same order as the simplest and least advanced of mankind, and that the ordinary man is the Sage's potential equal.[1] The Jesuit Le Comte, who went to China in the last quarter of the seventeenth century, comments on what he regards as the " very extraordinary " fact that the Chinese had never deified Confucius. It seemed " as if Heaven, that had given him birth for the reformation of manners, was unwilling that such a well-ordered life should, after his death, administer occasion of superstition and idolatry." [2]

One of the causes of the misunderstanding on this subject among foreigners is the existence of a temple-cult with its accompanying rituals. When a visitor from the West entered a *shêng miao*—a term meaning " temple of the Sage " rather than " holy temple "— and saw there the images or " spirit-tablets " of Confucius and his principal disciples, and still more when he enjoyed the rare privilege of beholding the stately ceremonies till recently carried out in spring and autumn under official auspices in every Confucian temple in China, it was difficult for him to avoid regarding the temple as the " heathen " equivalent of a church and the ritual observances as the " heathen " equivalent of a Christian service. In fact, however, such comparisons, if legitimate enough (apart from the disparaging connotation of " heathen ") in the case of Buddhist and Taoist temples, are not admissible in the case of temples of the Confucian cult. Confucius, be it repeated, is reverenced as a Sage and as pre-eminent among the founders of Chinese civilisation, he is not worshipped as a god.

Confucius and his disciples are not by any means the only illustrious members of the Chinese race who have received such reverence and in whose honour temples have been erected. The names of philosophers, generals, administrators, poets and many others are found among those on whom emperors have bestowed posthumous titles and dignities and in whose honour temples or shrines have been erected in their native districts or throughout the land. The bestowal of such honorific titles by imperial decree is often described by Western writers as canonisation ; and if we accept this description (which in my opinion is not quite appropriate) we may say that the persons so honoured have been elevated to a status analogous to that of sainthood. But no Confucian Chinese seriously believes, or has been expected to believe, that imperial decrees could turn men into gods, or that the emperor was endowed with the privilege of creating deities by a wave of his vermilion pencil.

It is true that some of the illustrious dead, such as Kuan Yü—a warrior of the third century A.D., often inaccurately described as the Chinese " god of war "— have been given titles that seem to confer the rank of divinity upon them, and that many such persons have been given places in the Taoist pantheon. The popular cults associated with such " gods " can hardly be regarded as other than religious. But no fate similar to that of Kuan Yü (more generally known as Kuan Ti or " god Kuan ") has befallen Confucius.[3]

It is unnecessary to enumerate the various posthumous honours and titles that have been conferred upon Confucius (and also upon three generations of his immediate ancestors) by the emperors of successive dynasties.[4] The last of them were bestowed on the Sage during the last decade of Manchu rule, and many foreigners have erroneously inferred that these were intended to elevate Confucius from the rank of mere humanity to that of divinity. Dr. H. A. Giles, rather surprisingly, seems to have shared this view ; for he declared that the Manchus had " foolishly elevated Confucius to the rank of a god."[5] Certainly it would have been a foolish proceeding if such had been the purpose of the edict to which Dr. Giles referred. But the object of the new honours was not to deify Confucius but to conciliate the mandarin-class who were outraged at the rapid westernisation of the educational system and to convince them that there was no intention on the part of the Throne to discard Confucianism or to remove Confucius from his supreme place in the moral and intellectual life of the nation. The position was accurately stated, only two or three years after the edict was issued, by the present bishop of Exeter, who happened to be in China at that time. After observing that on certain occasions all teachers and pupils in Government schools were required to bow before the tablet of Confucius, and that " missionaries hold that such action is not consistent with the Christian faith," he goes on to say that " several Chinese scholars, including a Christian, have indignantly denied that the kow-towing to the tablet of Confucius implies anything more than the respect due to the greatest thinker that China ever possessed. We had the privilege of being shown over Peking University by an extremely able and pleasant Chinese gentleman, a Christian. He showed us the tablet of Confucius and explained to us the ceremony. It must be owned that externally there was but little that one could associate with the idea of divinity. . . . The gentleman who showed us over strenuously denied that any of the pupils in Peking Government University could regard Confucius as God."

Lord William Gascoyne-Cecil goes on to say that he discussed this aspect of the matter with " an eminent missionary," who replied, " yes, but by a late edict they have made Confucius equal to heaven and earth, and so whatever doubts there were before have been resolved, and the Chinese Government has decreed to Confucius divine honour. I put this criticism to an able civil servant in the employ of the Chinese Government, and he answered that that decree was really intended to have the opposite effect. The Chinese are aware that they are as a matter of fact relegating Confucius to a secondary place in education, and they are therefore most anxious to propitiate the Confucian scholars."[6]

Lord William was correctly informed. The bestowal of high-sounding titles or honorary epithets in this and similar cases may be compared, not too inaptly, with the elevation to the peerage of an English statesman who wishes to breathe a more tranquil and serene atmosphere than that of the House of Commons. The missionary who by training and temperament has a keen scent for " idolatry " and its attendant horrors is apt to be too rigid and literal in his interpretation of " heathen " practices which do harm to none and give innocent satisfaction to many.

In the case of Confucius, not only have he and his ancestors received posthumous honours but his direct descendants have also shared his glory. The title (*kung*) of which the usual English equivalent is " duke," was first conferred upon the head of the family in the eleventh century of our era, and the rank was confirmed by succeeding dynasties. The republican Government declines to recognise it, but the present head of the family is still accorded the ducal title by all those who have remained faithful to the traditional usages. The actual title in full is *Yen Shêng Kung*, which may be translated " Duke of Extended Holiness," though as " Holiness " has a religious significance which hardly belongs to the Chinese term *shêng*, perhaps " Sagehood " is preferable. The present holder of the title is reputed to be the direct descendant of Confucius in the seventy-seventh generation. As Confucius is believed to have lived from 551 to 479 B.C., it will be seen that, even if we disregard the legends of Confucius's remote imperial ancestry, the family may claim to be nearly twenty-five centuries old. The father of the present duke, whose name was K'ung Ling-yi, was personally known to me and I enjoyed his hospitality in his ancestral mansion in the autumn of 1904.

Before the eleventh century, the honours of the family had varied to some extent according to the caprice of the reigning emperor, but the head of it always held the honorary rank of membership of the Hanlin Academy, a privilege which, it may be remarked, also belonged to the senior representative of the descendants of Mencius. The duke took precedence of the highest personages in the land after a limited number of the imperial princes. He was not, like the ministers of state, regarded as a servant (*ch'ên*) of the Throne but as an

F G

Imperial Guest (*k'o*). This was not in virtue of the
duke's patent of nobility but because he was regarded
as the living representative of the Master who was
the acknowledged Teacher of the Chinese race. According to a passage in the classical *Li Chi* (" Record of
Rites and Ceremonies ") there were " two men in the
realm whom the ruler cannot regard as his subjects.
One is the man who in the ritual sacrifices to the
dead personates the royal ancestors; the other is his
teacher."[7]

The duke's residence was and is at Ch'ü-Fou, the
little city of Shantung in which stands the greatest of
all the Confucian temples in China—the mother-
temple of Confucianism. Of this great building it is
the duke's duty and privilege to be the custodian. He
is also the guardian of the Sage's tomb, which lies in a
beautiful wooded graveyard outside the city.

It is perhaps worthy of remark that in the early days
of the revolutionary movement in China, the suggestion
was put forward that the Confucian duke, as the most
exalted of all persons of Chinese race, and as the
representative of the great Sage who was still held by
the vast majority of the Chinese people to be the ideal
man and the greatest of the founders or transmitters
of Chinese civilisation, should be placed at the head of
the State, either as first sovereign of a new and purely
Chinese dynasty or as first president of the Chinese
republic. The idea was dismissed by the revolutionary
leaders as fantastic, but the fact that it should have
been discussed, at least in unofficial circles, is an indication of the high prestige still enjoyed by the living

Ceiling of the Great Hall of the Confucian Temple at Ch'ü-Fou, showing autograph scrolls written by Emperors of China in praise of Confucius

representative of Confucius at the beginning of the revolutionary era.

It is not surprising that misunderstandings exist with regard to the nature of the homage rendered to Confucius, for there are Confucians of the present day who, if they do not go so far as to worship Confucius as a god, are at least anxious to give a definitely religious colouring to the ceremonies connected with his cult. Such persons, if asked whether Confucianism is a religion or not, would unhesitatingly answer " yes." They are participators in a modern movement, the main object of which is, or was, to emphasise the religious elements in the Confucian cult and to obtain official recognition for Confucianism in the written constitution of the republic as the state-religion or state-cult of China. Since 1924 the movement has subsided into quiescence, partly because there has been little talk in recent years about a written constitution but mainly because the new Nationalism, and the dominant cult of Sun Yat-sen with his " Three Principles " has overpowered the spirit of Old China and has deposed Confucius from his place of honour as the Teacher of the Chinese nation.

The motive underlying the movement to make Confucianism the state-religion was not a desire to raise Confucius from the rank of human sagehood to that of godhead but the belief that unless Confucianism were given the status of a religion, and placed first among the religions of the Chinese people, it would be

handicapped in its struggle against those rival forces—
including Christianity—which hoped or expected to
profit by its overthrow.[8]

The leaders of the movement class Confucianism
among the *tsung chiao*, a term which has come into
general use in modern times as the Chinese equivalent
of " religion."[9] But the great majority of Confucians,
who are not particularly interested in the question of
whether it is or is not a religion, prefer to speak simply
of *K'ung chiao* or *K'ung hsüeh*—"the teaching of K'ung."[10]

Even *K'ung chiao* and *K'ung hsüeh* are terms which
were rarely heard in Confucian circles till contact with
the West made it necessary to adopt a new phraseology,
and the former, at least, is by no means popular among
the learned. They prefer the ancient and familiar term
Ju chiao, which, if an English rendering is necessary,
means " the teaching or doctrine of scholars of the
orthodox tradition."[11]

The history of the term *Ju chiao* would repay study.
It is as old as the period of the Warring States (*Chan
Kuo*)—fifth and fourth centuries B.C.—and possibly
older, and it seems to have been applied to " orthodox "
scholars by their rivals of other schools as a term of
ridicule or contempt. It would appear that the followers
of Mo Ti or other unorthodox teachers were wont to
regard their orthodox rivals as cowardly and peace-
loving pedants, and used the term *ju* to express the
ideas of pedantry and timidity. But after the time
of Confucius, the great " transmitter " of orthodox
scholarship, the term began to be accepted by his
followers (perhaps in a spirit of humility) and therefore

gradually came to lose its original signification. From being a term of contempt it became one of honour and respect. Thus we do not find *Ju chiao* applied to the Confucian teachings in such early books of the canon as the *Ta Hsüeh* and *Chung Yung*, but in the book of Mencius (who lived 372–289 B.C.) it began to be so applied.[12]

Hence we find that the term *ju* underwent a change of meaning not unlike that which befell the words *Christian* and *Quaker*, which were originally used by pagans and non-Quakers as epithets of contempt or ridicule.[13]

Whatever may have been the original meaning of *Ju chiao* it certainly did not convey the idea of " religion." Nor can we say that the teachings of which Confucius spoke of himself as the " transmitter and not the founder " were primarily of a religious character. They were mainly concerned with ethical, political and social questions, and there is ample evidence that he never undertook or professed to present his disciples with solutions of spiritual problems.

This by no means implies that Confucius was indifferent to such problems or even that he was an agnostic. Critics may complain, and have complained, that *in rebus divinis* he was not sufficiently outspoken, that he failed to satisfy the curiosity of his followers on eschatological questions, formulated no creed, and did not define God or the divine attributes. They forget, perhaps, the wise saying that *un Dieu défini* is in danger of becoming *un Dieu fini*.[14] As St. Augustine said, "we can know what God is not ; we cannot know what He is."[15]

There is a passage in the canonical *Shu Ching* which ends with the words *yü Ti ch'i hsün*—" from God are these precepts." Dr. Legge's comment on this is " we must wish that the language of this paragraph had been more explicit."[16] Why should it have been more explicit if the writer meant no more and no less than what he said—that " these precepts are of divine origin " ? Similarly, commenting on a passage in *Mencius* in which God is mentioned, Dr. Legge very characteristically remarks that " it gives to T'ien [Heaven or God] a positive, substantial meaning, *though the personality of the Power is not sufficiently prominent.*"[17] If the headmaster of Eton was right when he said, as recently as June, 1933, that " there is no sort of reason why a Christian should hesitate to admit that he does not understand the ultimate nature of the Godhead,"[18] surely Confucius and his School cannot be held blameworthy for having refrained from discussing the Godhead in the sixth century B.C. Confucius lived in an age of gross superstition and of many crude and savage forms of religious belief. This is a truth which modern research into early Chinese civilisation is slowly bringing to light, and it is probable that the Sage's much-criticised reluctance to discuss the unseen world was largely due to his consciousness that what the great majority of his countrymen needed was less, rather than more, of what passed for religion in those days. He may have known that any dogmatic utterances which he might make on religious subjects would almost certainly be misunderstood or distorted, and he therefore tried to crush, rather than encourage, the luxuriance of the religious imagination of his country-men. It used to be a Western belief that the religion of the early Chinese was a pure and exalted monotheism. Much more probably it was a primitive polytheism based on nature-worship and associated with cruel and barbarous rites which continued to be practised among the unlettered masses long after they had fallen into discredit with the educated minority. That human sacrifices were not unknown may be gathered from the hints given by such stories as that told by Liu Hsiang about duke Ching of Ch'i.[19] The better-known incident of the prayer of Ch'êng T'ang in the mulberry grove, which has recently been a subject of scholarly research in China, points in the same direction.[20] From the *Tso Chuan* and other sources we learn that there was much witchcraft, and that in seasons of drought witches were sometimes treated with what we should regard as shocking barbarity. The period of the " royal sages," to which the Confucian School looked back as the golden age of civilisation and model rulership, is more likely to have been an age of barbarism, cruelty and gross forms of superstition, when human life was " nasty, brutish and short."

There are many passages in the canonical Confucian books which could be cited in illustration of the Master's deep religious feeling. One of the most striking, though it seems to have been misinterpreted by many Chinese and European commentators, is that which records his answer to someone who asked him to explain the meaning of a certain popular saying—" to propitiate the divinity of the cooking-stove is more effective than to propitiate the divinity of the inner rooms."

The saying seems to have conveyed an ironical suggestion that, although the cooking-stove divinity or " kitchen-god " was a humbler personage than the divinity who presided over the *penetralia*, he was likely to be of greater practical service to the family than his more august colleague, inasmuch as it was he who provided them with their " daily bread."

The answer of Confucius, as I read it, was a denial that anything was to be gained by worshipping or paying court to either of these small divinities, who were the creation of popular fancy and whose cult was mere superstition. " It is useless to pray to such as these," said Confucius in effect ; " address your prayers to God alone. If He rejects them there is no other deity to whom you may pray." In other words, there was only One fitting object of prayer.[21]

Nevertheless it is a common belief, especially among Western but also among some Chinese students of Confucian thought, that the attitude of Confucius towards spiritual matters was agnostic if not atheistic, and that the system of Confucius may best be described by the phrase applied to it by Dr. Hu Shih—" an agnostic humanism."[22] In proof of the Sage's agnosticism it is usual to quote such passages as that in which he is said to have recommended his followers to " devote themselves to their duties as men, and to respect spiritual beings but keep aloof from them."[23]

All that Confucius seems to have meant by this is correctly stated by Dr. Legge, whose testimony is all the more valuable because it comes from one whose bias often prevented him from doing justice to Confucius. The Sage's advice, as Dr. Legge says, was this— " attend to what are plainly human duties and do not be superstitious "[24]—a very necessary warning to the Chinese of the Confucian or any other age, and by no means the same thing as advising them to hold religion in contempt.

The alleged agnosticism of Confucius is also supposed to be illustrated in his reply to a disciple who questioned him about death and the spirit-world. " If you have not learned how to fulfil your duties to living men, how can you hope to fulfil those you owe to the dead? If you do not know about life, what can you know about death? " This passage occurs in the *Chia Yü*, a book of which the authenticity is very doubtful, and in any case the words cannot legitimately be regarded as proving that Confucius was irreligious.[25] They are not incompatible with a sincere belief in the existence of a spiritual world; though if authentic they show that in the opinion of Confucius a curiosity about the next world and even a sincere devotion to religious beliefs and practices did not absolve men from the duties and obligations that lay immediately before them in this mundane sphere.

There is abundant evidence that this has generally been the view of orthodox Confucianism. The same lesson is taught in the following remarkable little anecdote which was placed on record several centuries before the existing *Chia Yü* was written.

" A certain feudal prince, perceiving the approaching ruin of his principality, sent for his chief priest with the intention of punishing him. ' You,' he said, ' must have been niggardly in your sacrifices and perfunctory in your ritual duties, and so you are responsible for the catastrophe that is befalling the State. What have you to say ? ' The chief priest replied as follows. ' Once there was a prince of this State who possessed only ten war-chariots. But it was not his lack of military equipment that made him sorrowful : he lamented only when he found himself lacking in virtue. Now you, my prince, possess ten times the number of chariots that he had, yet it is not your lack of virtue that troubles you but your lack of war-material. Your ships and chariots make a brave show indeed, but your State is overloaded with taxation. Under the weight of their burdens, your people have a deep sense of wrong and invoke curses upon you. Under such conditions, do you suppose my prayers can be of any benefit to the State ? If benedictions are profitable, it must be equally true that maledictions are harmful. One man prays for you and the whole nation curses you. How can you expect the prayers of one to prevail over the curses of tens of thousands ? If the State goes to ruin, why blame the inefficacy of my prayers ? '

" The prince was shamed into silence."[26]

The Confucian attitude towards the less harmful forms of superstition was one of scepticism coupled with gentle tolerance, and use was often made of them to inculcate moral lessons. Many of the popular beliefs in China as in other lands were connected with the movements of planets and comets. One of Liu Hsiang's instructive little stories is the following :

"A comet made its appearance in the State of Ch'i. The marquis of Ch'i ordered his high-priest to carry out a propitiatory ceremony. The minister Yen intervened, saying, 'That would be a useless proceeding. God cannot be humbugged with mere priestcraft. When he puts a celestial sign in the sky, his purpose is to incline the hearts of princes to refrain from doing the evil things that displease him. If you are not conscious of having done wrong, a ceremony of exorcism or propitiation is unnecessary. If you have done wrong, how can such a ceremony right it ? Why fear a comet if you have done nothing to deserve misfortune ? ' This exhortation had the desired effect, and the marquis cancelled the ceremony."[27]

If we wished to prove that Confucianism is a religion it would be easy to select passages from the Confucian classics which would make our case a strong one. There are pages in the classics which are not only religious in character but point to an exalted ideal of what religion means. The following example comes from a remarkable tract called the *Chi T'ung*—"A General Account of Religious Ceremonial "—which is believed to date from the fourth century B.C. In my translation I have rendered the word *chi* by " religion."

Its general signification is "sacrificial offering" or "oblation." The Chinese character symbolises a hand holding a piece of sacrificial meat, or the offering of a sacrifice that brings divine influences down to earth.

"Religion is not a thing that comes to man from without. It has its origin in his innermost being and is born in his heart. When emotion stirs the heart there is an outward manifestation of it, and that, when ordered aright, is ritual. Only men of virtue can give adequate expression to the meaning of religion. Religion as manifested by them brings happiness, but it is not the happiness in material things such as the world seeks. . . . In their religion there is sincerity and truth, straightforwardness and reverence. The proper sacrifices are offered, accompanied by the proper rites and by tranquillising music. Each season has its appropriate ritual. Those who are truly religious have no ulterior object in their sacrifices and seek no reward."[28]

Whatever conclusion we may come to as to the right of Confucianism to be called a religion, we may safely say that it possesses two characteristics which most of us would agree are essential to religion—namely, a sound and workable system of ethics and an acknowledgment of the existence of a divine order. As to the excellence of its ethics, I think there should be no serious disagreement, although critics may assert that it ascribes an excessive value to filial piety and lays insufficient stress on some of the other virtues. Perhaps we should be justified in putting the matter in this way—that there is no ethical principle recognised in the West as valid that is not explicit or implicit in the Confucian teachings, and no " Christian " virtue that could not be preached from a Confucian text ; and that in Confucian ethics the Chinese people have a strong and sure foundation on which to build the moral life.

Moreover, if it be true that some ethical ideas are overstressed and others understressed, it may be affirmed that there is nothing in the nature of Confucianism as a living system that precludes whatever adjustments of ethical values may be considered necessary in the light of advancing human knowledge and growing human experience.

The excellence of Confucian ethics was more generously recognised by some of the earlier Christian missionaries than by most of their modern successors. The Jesuit missionary Le Comte, who was by no means an undiscriminating admirer of things Chinese—the Chinese language was to him an abomination—had nothing but high praise for Confucius as a man and for his ethical teachings.

" There is scarce anything can be added either to his zeal, or to the purity of his morality, they were so superlative. Methinks he sometimes speaks like a doctor of the new law, rather than like a man that was brought up in the corruption of the law of nature : and that which persuades me that hypocrisy had no share in what he said is that his actions never belied his maxims. In fine, his gravity and mildness

in the use of the world, his rigorous abstinence (for
he passed for the soberest man of the empire), his
contempt of the good things of the world, that con-
tinual attention and watchfulness over his actions,
and then (which we find not among the sages of
antiquity) his humility and modesty, would make
a man apt to judge that he was not a mere philosopher formed by reason, but a man inspired by God
for the reformation of this new world."[29]

Le Comte, of course, and all his successors, would have
been quick to add that "ethics is not enough"; and even
if we grant, as we must, that Confucius neither ignored
nor despised the things of the spirit, it must be admitted
that he laid down " no definite rules for the guidance
of explorers in the spiritual realm."[30] This is why
multitudes of spiritually-minded Chinese have found
Confucianism adequate as a rule of life but inadequate
as a guide to the spiritual world, and have therefore
sought additional consolation and enlightenment, such
as Confucius could not give, in Buddhism, Taoism, or
(in modern times) Christianity.[31] Dr. H. O. Taylor
has somewhere described Confucianism (with its
vita activa) and Taoism (with its *vita contemplativa*) as
the Martha and Mary of China ; and the comparison
is a good one. On the other hand there has always
been a still larger number of educated Chinese who
have found in Confucianism all the ethical and spiritual
nourishment of which they are consciously in need,
either because their minds are predominantly of the
" once-born " or this-worldly type or because they are

content, for the present, with the glimpses that Confucius has given them of the spiritual world and are willing to await in patience the fuller knowledge that may come to them when their work in the world is done.[32]

The very fact that Confucius refused to dogmatise on subjects that did not come within the scope of his teaching or concerning which he did not profess to have access to exceptional sources of information, is sufficient in the eyes of many people to justify a negative answer to the question of whether Confucianism is or is not a religion. Perhaps they are right. It is not a question which has caused much debate in China itself, or rather it did not do so until Confucianism came into conflict or competition with Christianity and had to make some attempt to define its own position more accurately than had formerly been necessary.[33] That is why we find one school of contemporary Confucian thought asserting that Confucianism is a religion, and another asserting with equal vigour that it is not. The controversy is one which has been created by contact with the West, and even at the present day it is one to which the great body of Confucians are indifferent.[34]

A Protestant missionary of a generation ago—Dr. J. Edkins—made the very significant and I think true remark that " when the evidence of a new religion is presented " to the Chinese " they at once refer it to a moral standard, and give their approval with the utmost readiness if it passes the test. *They do not ask whether it is divine but whether it is good.*"[35]

I think an educated Chinese, if pressed on this subject, would heartily agree with Dr. A. N. Whitehead, who has reminded us—if, since the days of Lucretius, we need reminding—that " religion is not always a good thing ; it may be a very bad thing."[36] The Confucian feels fully justified in asking the question that Dr. Edkins cited as typical. He does not ask whether a religion is divine but whether it is good ; feeling satisfied that if it be good it will be divine enough for human needs, whereas if it be divine without being good, its divinity may have its uses in heaven but has none in the world of living men.[37]

It is not surprising that differences of opinion should exist both among Confucians and non-Confucians as to how the Confucian system should be labelled, seeing that Western scholars are similarly unable to agree among themselves as to what constitute the essentials of religion. We have lately been told by several writers that Communism is a religion. If they are right, it would surely be unfair to deny that Confucianism deserves to be placed in the same category.[38] Whatever else Confucianism may or may not be, it is certainly neither atheistical nor materialistic, whereas Communism is both.[39]

The theory that Communism is a religion has been defended on the ground that it is a supra-rational cause for which men will die, and that such a cause is a religion. If that be the ultimate test, Confucianism passes it with ease, for it has had its martyrs and many have willingly courted or suffered death for its sake. One of these was a man named Ch'ien T'ang. I have already mentioned the historical fact that the first emperor of the Ming dynasty inaugurated his reign by degrading the spirit-tablet of Mencius from its place of honour in the Confucian Temple, because he was alleged to have spoken disrespectfully of monarchs. An indignant Confucian had the temerity to send a memorial to the Throne vehemently protesting against the imperial decree. The emperor promptly ordered him to be put to death. Just as the bowman was about to discharge the fatal arrow, Ch'ien T'ang (who was one of the highest ministers of state) threw himself with bared breast in front of the condemned man and received the arrow. As he lay wounded on the ground, he said, " If I die for Mencius I do so gladly and with pride." Hearing of the incident the emperor repented of his action, released and pardoned the condemned man, and sent court-physicians to attend to the wound of the courageous Ch'ien T'ang, who in due course recovered. The spirit-tablet of Mencius was triumphantly reinstated in the temple of the Confucian cult, and as " Second Sage " (a title which, however, he did not receive till 1530) he has since occupied a place in the Confucian system subordinate only to that of the great Sage himself.

If I were called upon to define Confucianism I should be inclined to set aside the question of whether it is a religion or not and call it a Life. We are often told nowadays that Christianity is not a creed but a Life. I do not deny the right of Christianity to be so described, I merely make the same claim for Confucianism on

Gc

grounds which I believe to be at least as strong as those on which the Christian claim rests.[40]

The same claim may be and has been made for other systems besides Christianity and Confucianism. Of Stoicism and Epicureanism Dr. W. R. Inge has said that they "were both, first and foremost, attitudes towards life ; they claimed to regulate conduct in every particular." He also shows that for the Socrates of Plato's *Republic* the proper teaching of philosophy was "how a man may spend his life to the best advantage."[41] Buddhism, too, is a path of life, and the very meaning of the name of Taoism is enough to show us that it was primarily a " Way."

Humanity is surely entitled to congratulate itself on this most striking fact, that if the great ethico-religious systems of the world can find unanimity in nothing else, they can at least find it in this—that each aims at being a Way of Life. It justifies a hope and a belief that even if the " ways " are many, and some are more circuitous than others, they all lead finally to the same *Civitas Dei*.

To confine ourselves to Confucianism, we may add, I think, that it is not only a Life but an Art. Mr. Aldous Huxley, in an eloquent passage, tells us that people will accept the religious beliefs and rites of their age and country " not because they imagine the statements to be true or the rules and rites to be divinely dictated, but simply because they have discovered experimentally that to live in a certain ritual rhythm, under certain ethical restraints, and as if certain metaphysical doctrines were true, is to live nobly, with style." He adds, " Every art has its conventions, which every artist must accept. The greatest, the most important of the arts is living."[42]

Mr. Aldous Huxley has, I think, expressed in his own fine language a discovery which Confucius and his School made more than two thousand years ago.

I am glad to welcome as a fellow-supporter of the view that Confucianism is pre-eminently an art and a life, another great thinker of to-day who, without possessing first-hand knowledge of Chinese culture, is happily endowed with the gifts that have enabled him to discern its spirit. I refer to Mr. Havelock Ellis. He believes that Greece and China are the two countries that have had the finest civilisations. " The wisest and most recognisably greatest practical philosophers of both these lands," he says, " have believed that the whole of life, even government, is an art of definitely like kind with the other arts, such as that of music or the dance."[43] He was delighted to make the discovery that in China " life was regulated by music and ceremony " ; and he declares that " it is in music, and the joy and peace that accompany music, that it all ends." He adds that " it is also in music that it all begins. For the sphere in which ceremonies act is Man's external life ; his internal life is the sphere of music."[44]

I hope in the next section to show that this is, as far as it goes, a correct account of the spirit of Confucian China.

CHAPTER VIII

MUSIC AND CEREMONIAL IN THE CONFUCIAN SYSTEM

Even the briefest sketch of the Confucian system must find room for some account of Music and Ceremonial. The two (*Yüeh* and *Li*) have been linked together from the earliest days of Confucian speculation. According to the canonical tradition, Confucius was from his early youth a deeply-interested student of rites and ceremonies, so that he came to be known as a *Chih Li chih jên*—" one who knows the rites." As evidence of his enthusiasm for music it is hardly necessary to do more than refer to the famous passage in the *Lun Yü* in which it is stated that " When the Master was in the state of Ch'i he heard the Shao music and for three months ' did not know the taste of meat.' "[1] Various interpretations of this remarkable statement have been offered, and we need not take the trouble to examine them. We know, however, from another passage that the music by which Confucius was so deeply moved, and which was attributed to the perhaps mythical emperor Shun (one of the ideal sage-kings of early Chinese history), was considered by Confucius to be " perfectly beautiful and also perfectly good." Of another kind of music (the *Wu*) his opinion was that it was " perfectly beautiful but not perfectly good "—the reason being that it was martial in character and therefore suggestive of the angry passions aroused by war.[2] That he possessed a technical knowledge of the ritual music of his time—now, alas, lost—may be gathered from various passages in the canon, and it is also clear that he took a personal part in reforming the music of his native state.[3]

Now the important point—as we can see from the Sage's partial disapproval of the music of *Wu*—is that music was regarded by him as being intimately associated both with ceremonial and with public and private morals. " If a man does not possess the virtues that should govern his relations with his fellow-men," said Confucius, " what concern has he with *Li*—Ceremonial—or with *Yüeh*—Music ? "[4]

Elsewhere he uttered an equally remarkable saying which I translate as follows—" Poetry is what gives the first stimulus to the character ; Ceremonial is what gives it stability ; Music is what brings it to full development."[5]

In Mencius we find utterances of a similar kind. He, too, finds an intimate connection between virtuous thought and feeling and their outward manifestation in properly regulated music and ceremonial.[6]

" It is the duty of the minister in charge of education," said the Chinese philosopher Hsün K'uang more than two thousand years ago, " to prohibit any grossness in songs, to regulate musical performances by the season, and to see that the music of our cultured land is not corrupted by the uncouth cacophonies of the

barbarians "[7] : from which we may surmise that
Hsün K'uang, as well as Confucius and Mencius, would
have abstained from bestowing his benediction on
jazz.[8]

What the Confucian music was like we do not know ;
the music that accompanied the ceremonial of later
ages was an attempt to reproduce it, but it is doubtful
whether it bears more than a remote resemblance to
the music which to Confucius was not only beautiful
to the ear and mind but had an important bearing on
morals.

A very striking parallel may be drawn between the
Confucian ideas about the ethical significance of music
and those of the Greeks. We know how important a
part was assigned to music in Plato's educational plan.
" He hopes by its aid," as Jowett observes, " to make
the lives of his youthful scholars harmonious and
gracious, and to implant in their souls true conceptions
of good and evil." This is entirely in the spirit of
Confucius, as is also the remark that " where there is
license in music there will be anarchy in the state."[9]

Plato said that " the introduction of a new kind of
music must be shunned as imperilling the whole state ;
since styles of music are never disturbed without
affecting the most important political institutions."
This was Confucius's view too, though he did not
mean by it that music was a static thing and not subject to the laws of growth and change. The *Shuo Yüan*
quotes a saying of Confucius—" for modifying and
improving the manners and customs of the people
nothing is better than music ; just as for ensuring

peace to the rulers and tranquillity to the people nothing is better than right ceremonial."[10]

Irving Babbitt, whose sympathetic comprehension of Oriental ideals was noteworthy, was right when he observed that " Confucius and the Chinese sages were if anything even more concerned than Plato and Aristotle with the ethical quality of music."[11]

Confucius, whose years were from 551 to 479 B.C., was in all probability a contemporary of the Buddha and died only about half a century before Plato was born. Had Greece, India and China been in communication with one another at that wonderful epoch of the world's history, when all those three great countries, each in complete ignorance of the doings of the others, were simultaneously producing religions and philosophies and constructing brilliant scientific hypotheses, the influence of which will never cease to be felt as long as the human race endures, how inconceivably glorious for the cultural history of mankind might have been the result of the intermingling of their greatest minds ![12]

As there is no doubt of the great importance ascribed by Confucius to ritual and ceremonial music, the question may be asked whether all popular music was included in his sweeping condemnation of the music that was " barbarous " and subversive of sound morals. There is no doubt, I think, that he had a genuine appreciation of music as such and loved the folk-songs and other simple music of the people provided that it was not the ancient Chinese equivalent of jazz. His attitude towards genuine folk-music may perhaps be surmised from a delightful anecdote preserved in the canonical *Analects*.

Confucius, we are told, was sitting one day with four of his disciples and asked each of them what he would do if he were in a position of authority or free to do what he liked. The first, a self-confident and ambitious young man, said he would like to be the minister of a weak State which was threatened by many internal and external dangers. Within three years, he said, he would make it a strong State inhabited by a wise and intrepid people. The second disciple said, more modestly, that if he were a minister he might perhaps succeed, in three years' time, in providing the people with enough to live on, but that as for teaching them the essentials of a true civilisation (music and ceremonial) he would have to leave that to a greater man than himself. The third disciple, still more diffident about his own capacities, said he would be content if he might serve as acolyte in the State temples and learn from observation how the rites ought to be conducted. Finally the Master turned to the fourth disciple, whose name was Tien, and put the same question to him.

"Tien up to that moment had been thrumming his lute. He laid it aside, with the strings still vibrating, and said, as he rose to his feet, ' My ambitions are altogether different from theirs.' ' Never mind,' said the Master ; ' tell me what they are.'

"' It is near the end of spring,' said Tien. ' What I should like to do would be to change into light raiment, join a little company of youths and boys, go

with them to bathe in the Yi river, enjoy the breeze
and dance among the sylvan shrines, and come home
singing.'
   " The Master sighed, and said, ' Tien, I feel just
like you.' "13

If this little tale proves nothing else it seems to show
that Confucius was very far from being the austere
pedant that he is sometimes supposed to have been.
But how precious to us would have been a record of the
tune that Tien, unchidden by his Master, had been
thrumming on his lute, and of the songs that he and
his companions would have sung on the way home
from their picnic on the banks of the Yi !
   The word *Li*, which in the Confucian canon is
commonly associated with *Yüeh* (music), is, like many
other Chinese classical terms, baffling in its elusiveness.
I have used " ceremonial," but if that is inadequate
still more so are the terms " etiquette " and " politeness." Yet the word is of supreme importance, and
without a proper understanding of what it means we
shall never enter into the heart of Confucianism. Legge
translates it " the rules of propriety." This rendering
has caused difficulty to many Western students of
the Chinese classics and has helped to foster among
Europeans the utterly false impression that Confucianism is a system of petty social regulations, stiff
and meaningless conventions.
   Dr. H. A. Giles, till recently the distinguished professor of Chinese at Cambridge, gives " ceremony " as
his primary rendering ; and also gives " etiquette,

politeness, presents and offerings."[14] Certainly it means all these, and more. He gives another and deeper meaning which he isolates from the others : " Worship." There he shows us *Li* in its religious aspect —for that it had some connection with religion is obvious from the very construction of its written symbol. Dr. Giles also, very properly, gives as his first illustrative example of the use and meaning of *Li* the phrase *Li chê so i ch'ing mao*, which he translates " Ceremony is the outward expression of inward feeling." This indeed is what *Li* is : and we can go further, for in the *Li Chi* or " Record of Rites and Ceremonies " we are told that " Ceremonial "—" Ritual " would be a better rendering here—" is rooted in heaven and comes to florescence in humanity."[15]

Bertrand Russell's perspicacity failed him when he declared that the " writings " of Confucius are " largely occupied with trivial points of etiquette " and that his " main concern is to teach people how to behave correctly on various occasions."[16] Little wonder is it that he confessed his inability to " appreciate the merits of Confucius." Nevertheless he must have had misgivings as to the correctness of his own judgment, which after all was presumably based on English translations, the best of which leave much to be desired ; for he goes on to say that the Confucian system " certainly has succeeded in producing a whole nation possessed of exquisite manners and perfect courtesy."

" Exquisite manners and perfect courtesy " ! I wish we could assert that these words are as true of the

New China that has been trying to throw away its old traditions and break up the foundations of its cultural heritage, as they undoubtedly were of the Old China that is passing away. Confucian China had a whole-hearted belief in the truth that is so delightfully expressed in the famous Wykehamist motto " Manners makyth man." Republican China, or at least that large and influential section of it which regards Confucianism and all it stands for in manners and morals as outworn and effete, seeks its ideals elsewhere.

Let me translate some passages from the " Record of Rites and Ceremonies " which illustrates the Confucian attitude.

" Those who were the flower of civilisation in olden times had no need to explain their views by making speeches ; all they had to do was to express themselves in music and ceremonial. . . . Men who are the flower of civilisation in our own time and who know how to express themselves in music and ceremonial, have the qualities of statesmanship. . . . But when the moral nature is unstable, music and ceremony are practised in vain."[17]

To-day we do not hear much in China about music and ceremonial and their intimate association with the moral nature. This is certainly, in China—and elsewhere—an epoch of moral instability ; we need not be surprised, then, that ceremonies and music, if practised at all, are " practised in vain."

A few words must be said of the significance of both music and ceremonial in the Court-life of Old China.

Something of this significance may be understood when we have studied the *Yüeh Chi* or "Record of Music," which is one of the books of the *Li Chi*. The date of this important chapter in China's classical literature is now contested, but as it stands it is one of the most fascinating documents in the language. It explains the close connection that the Chinese believed to exist between music, ceremonial, morals and the art of government. The following extracts, which I have attempted to translate with due regard to the spirit as well as the letter of the Chinese original, may help to make this clear.

"All ceremonies, music and laws have a single aim, which is to train the character and to make good government possible. . . . Between the ballads and the music of the people and the character of their government there is an intimate connection . . . the five notes of the scale symbolise the monarch, the ministers of state, the people, public administration, and the materials to be used in government. If there be no disorder or irregularity in the musical scale, there will be no lack of harmony in the State. . . . The common people know what tunes are, but it takes a *chün tzŭ* (a gentleman, a man of taste and refinement) to know what music is. . . . He who understands both ceremonies and music is the civilised man . . . When ceremonies, music, and laws are interacting harmoniously, there is nothing to prevent the realisation of true kingly government. . . . Music comes from within, ceremonies from without . . . if music be

allowed to have its full results, the mind will cease to
be dissatisfied and restless ; if ceremonies are allowed
to have their full results, men will be at peace with
one another . . . there will be no oppressive government, the feudal princes will cease to rebel and will be
received as honoured guests at Court ; there will be
no occasion for war, no need for harsh punishments ;
the people will have no complaints, the Son of
Heaven (i.e. the emperor) will have no cause for
wrath. Let these conditions be realised and there
will be universal music throughout the land. . . .
Music reproduces the harmonious interaction between heaven and earth ; ceremonies reproduce the
results of that harmony. . . . It is an old saying—
' where joy is, there is music.' . . . Virtue is natural to
man and grows as a tree grows : music is its blossoming. . . . Ceremonies and music partake of the nature of
both heaven and earth. Their influence reaches to
heaven and to spiritual beings; they bring the divine
down to earth and raise humanity to heaven."[18]

We might almost suspect Dryden of having surrepti-
tiously taken lessons in Chinese and consulted the
Yüeh Chi before he too set himself to extol the magical
power of music :

> *He raised a mortal to the skies,*
> *She drew an angel down.*[19]

*Virtue is natural to man and grows as a tree grows : music is
its blossoming.* In this and many other passages in the
Yüeh Chi we seem to be in contact with Greek thought

expressed in Chinese phraseology : for as Lowes Dickinson told us, the Greeks did not regard virtue as " a hard conformity to a law felt as alien to the national character ; it was the free expression of a beautiful and harmonious soul."[20] The same writer had ancient Greece in his mind, but he might have been referring to Confucian China, when he wrote these words : " that moral character should be attributed to the influence of music is only one and perhaps the most striking illustration " of a " general identification by the Greeks of the ethical and the aesthetic standards."[21]

The emperor himself was regarded as the apex of this wonderful ideal system of music and ritual.

" The Son of Heaven "—I am now translating from another part of the *Li Chi*—" is one of the members of a triad, of which the other two are the divine powers of heaven and earth. . . . Thus when he sits enthroned, all things are ordered in conformity with the highest principles of love and wisdom and their outward manifestations in ceremonies and right conduct. When he entertains his ministers, he hears the chanting of national songs and sacred hymns. . . .[22] Walking, he moves to the music of the precious stones suspended from his girdle. Driving in his chariot, he moves to the music of his horses' bells, and thus no evil or unworthy thoughts find lodgment in his mind. . . .[23] Thus fathers are brought into harmony with their sons, rulers with their subjects, and love unites the peoples of all the feudal states. Such were the purposes that guided the

Image of CONFUCIUS in the Great Hall of the Confucian Temple
at Ch'ü-Fou

ancient kings when they created their music. . . . Thus it was that under the ancient kings music and ceremonial reached their highest development."[24]

In several of these and many similar passages we perceive the deep moral significance which the Chinese attached to beautiful sounds and orderly ceremonies. Here is another example, taken from Mencius.

" I can judge of a country's government from the nature of its rites and ceremonies ; I can judge of its prince's virtue from the nature of its music."[25]

This passage, taken from the book of the " Second Sage " of Confucianism, receives amplification in the following quotation from the *Li Yün*.

" The Son of Heaven in the austerity of his virtue moves to the sound of music, his princely vassals in their relations with him and with one another move in obedience to the right ceremonial, the officers of state maintain the dignity of their several positions, each in his proper order, their subordinates are inspired with mutual trust and confidence, harmony reigns among the people and throughout the land all is well."[26]

When we read that the prince and the great officers of state " should never lay aside their girdles of pendant jade-stones without good reason," we may fail to understand the meaning of such a rule until we learn that " the jade-stones symbolised their participation in the moral life,"[27] and the moral life was not for a moment to be abandoned.

" Music and ceremonial," we are told elsewhere, " must never be neglected. With the mastery of music comes the proper regulation of heart and mind, hence it is no difficult matter to ensure the right development of human nature in accordance with justice, gentleness and good faith. With that development comes joy, and after joy comes lasting tranquillity. He who maintains himself in this state of joyous tranquillity is in harmony with heaven and with the spiritual world. Beholding in his nature something spiritual, his fellow-men have limitless trust in him even though he make no promises ; recognising in him something divine, they regard him with awe, even though he never fail in gentleness. . . . Similarly, when he has mastered ceremonial, and through it has learned to govern movement and action, he acquires gravity and good manners. So endowed, he is regarded with deep respect. With heart full of harmony and joy he keeps aloof from all that is mean and treacherous. . . . His inner self is ruled by music, his outer self by ceremony : hence his moral nature is a symphony, and manifests itself outwardly in gracious courtesy."[28]

Such being the Confucian theory of music and ritual or ceremonial, it is not surprising that both were of supreme importance in the imperial court. They dramatised the ideal relationship between a wise and good ruler and his subjects. The Chinese monarch was the intermediary between Earth and Heaven, that is to say between his people and God. Through the proper use of music and ceremonial he was believed to maintain equipoise and harmony between the divine and the human. As representative of God on earth, as the " Son of Heaven "—*T'ien Tzŭ*—he sat enthroned in a great hall known as the palace of Cloudless Heaven (*Ch'ien Ch'ing Kung*) ; behind that building was another —the Palace of Tranquil Earth (*K'un Ning Kung*) ; and between the two palaces of Heaven and Earth was the *Chiao T'ai Tien*—the " Hall of the Blending of the Great Creative Forces "—where the divine and earthly powers of the universe intermingled and reacted in perfect harmony.[29]

In all the foregoing there is much that may at first sight seem childish or fantastic, but rightly understood it contains both truth and beauty. It is not quite accurate to say, with Lowes Dickinson, that " with the Greek civilisation beauty perished from the world " ; or that " never again has it been possible for man to believe that harmony is in fact the truth of all existence."[30] The Chinese believed it in an age that was contemporary with that of Periclean Greece, and they have not quite ceased to believe it yet. And indeed the same truth has been glimpsed elsewhere, if not by whole peoples at least by their poets, who have recognised that " the language of intuition and mysticism is rhyme and rhythm, as the truest expression of the spirit of man is music."[31]

Hc

Nay, what is nature's
Self, but an endless
Strife towards music,
   Euphony, rhyme ?

Trees in their blooming,
Tides in their flowing,
Stars in their circling,
   Tremble with song.

God on his throne is
Eldest of poets :
Unto His measures
   Moveth the whole.[32]

Large numbers of *mo-têng* Chinese, as we have already
learned, believe that Confucianism is incompatible
with a democratic form of government. They think that
so long as Confucianism is allowed to exist there will be
an ever-present danger of a revival of monarchic hopes
and ideas. The main reason generally given for this
belief is that Confucius taught the duty of loyalty
to the sovereign. That, as we have seen, is a wholly
inadequate reason. But there is another and perhaps
stronger reason of which revolutionary China may be
only subconsciously aware and which I have never
seen discussed in anti-Confucian propaganda. It is
that in a democracy there is no room for " music
and ceremonial " in the traditional Chinese sense,
and that the mystical ideas associated with them in
classical China would be a laughable absurdity in a

progressive modern State. When in imagination we contemplate the stately ceremonial of court and temple in Old China, based as it was on the antique symbolism of the classical tradition, it is difficult to see how it could be successfully adapted to republican institutions borrowed from Europe and America. Presidential and parliamentary elections are not always regulated by cosmic laws of beauty and rhythm, not always even in obedience to earthly laws of dignity and decorum. The hooting of motor-cars is but a sorry substitute for the rhythmic jingle of jade-pendants and chariot-bells. It is doubtful whether cabinet-ministers invariably regard their portfolios as "symbols of their participation in the moral life"; and although they may, not infrequently, listen to " the chanting of national songs and sacred hymns," it may be questioned whether they habitually adapt their movements to the music of the spheres.

It must be admitted that even in the best and happiest days of Old China, human life was not always, if ever, an earthly reproduction of a divine symphony. It was not true, even of the wisest and most conscientious of Confucian statesmen, that their " outer selves " were always regulated by ceremony and their " inner selves " by music. But the ideal was one which was of vital significance, and was certainly not without practical results of profound value, for the Chinese people ; and if it were never wholly realisable in a world where the natural goodness of human nature was too often cramped and soiled by an evil environment, it was an ideal which the best of Chinese rulers and scholars never lost sight of, and which has been a creative force throughout all the ages of Chinese civilisation.[33]

Someone has said that religion was born among mankind at the moment when the first musical instrument was invented. A sympathetic understanding of the *Yüeh Chi* and of several other books of the *Li Chi* should convince us that Confucianism stands on the threshold of religion, and that the door leading to the mysteries within stands open. Truth and Goodness—these, it is generally acknowledged, receive in the Confucian system the reverence that must be accorded to them in every religious system or philosophy that deserves the name. Less fully has it been recognised that similar honour has been paid by Confucianism to Beauty. *Yüeh* and *Li*—Music and Ceremonial—are terms often used in combination (*Li-Yüeh*) to denote " civilisation " in its richest florescence. Together they reveal to us the homage rendered by Confucianism to all that is beautiful. Beauty, Goodness and Truth—these are for Confucianism the ultimate values, the basis of the Confucian interpretation of life, the key to the Confucian philosophy of the spirit. Surely we of the Western world should rejoice in our spiritual kinship with a Chinese sage, who more than two thousand years ago illumined his world with teachings which some of our Western sages have since taught in living words of their own and which have not lost their freshness and validity for either the Eastern or the Western world to-day.[34]

CHAPTER IX

FORTUNES OF CONFUCIANISM IN ANCIENT AND MODERN TIMES

DURING its long history of more than two thousand years—far more if we accept the Master's own statement that he was " a transmitter and not a maker "— the system to which we give the rather unsatisfactory name of Confucianism has undergone great vicissitudes. In its early days it was only one among several competing systems ; and three centuries after the time of Confucius it was nearly extinguished by the catastrophe known to history as " the burning of the books and the burying-alive of the scholars "—concisely expressed in the four Chinese words *fên shu k'êng ju*.

The story of that grim episode has often been told. When the ruler of the semi-barbarian state of Ch'in, in the far west of modern China, succeeded, in the middle of the third century B.C., in subduing all the Chinese feudal princes and bringing the whole empire under unified control, he conceived the idea—or rather his minister Li Ssŭ conceived it for him—of blotting out all memory of past ages and inaugurating a new era of which he himself was to be recognised for ever as the illustrious founder. This scheme was unworkable so long as the scholars of the empire— the dons of Old China—persisted in babbling, in the way dons will babble, about the classics and the ancient sages, and held up to the admiration of the " Young China " of that day the great deeds and sayings attributed to various holy kings of a former epoch. His method of dealing with the situation was as simple as it was drastic. He made a holocaust of all existing literature with the exception of books on the subjects of medicine and divination and the history of his native State of Ch'in ; and when the fraternity of scholars ventured to protest against this destruction of all that they held precious, he collected more than four hundred and sixty of them and caused them to be buried alive.

Upon himself he bestowed the title of Shih Huang-Ti, which means " The First Emperor," and he hoped either that he would live for ever, in which case the need for a second emperor would never arise, or, as a less satisfactory alternative, that he would be succeeded by an endless line of imperial descendants. Neither of these rosy hopes was realised. The elixirs of life, of which he is said to have sampled many, failed to release him from the common lot of mankind ; and the son who succeeded him on the throne was the second and last monarch of a dynasty which was to have endured for ever.

I used to think that the story of the burning of the books was a greatly exaggerated account of a more or less trifling incident, or that it had been invented by later scholars to account for the sudden appearance of books written by themselves under the name of real or fictitious authors of past ages for the purpose of giving an air of reality to the Utopias of their own imaginations. But events which have taken place during the past year or two in a country situated not ten thousand miles from England have led me to revise my old belief that the burning of books on a large scale under official sanction and encouragement, in the hope of obliterating a past which it was considered desirable to forget, was an act which no ruler of a civilised State could bring himself to carry out.[1]

I must admit that I did not take so grave a view of the burying of the scholars. Human life has been so often treated with contempt, both in ancient and in modern times, and in all parts of the world, that the mere execution of four hundred and sixty Chinese dons—who had probably shown themselves very refractory and conservative, as is often the way with dons— seemed a matter of relative insignificance. Besides, dons who are consigned to pits, even bottomless ones, can be replaced ; whereas books once destroyed—in the days when each copy had to be written laboriously by hand—were apt to be lost for ever. In these days of the printing-press it is easy to regard a public burning of books under official auspices with amused contempt, or perhaps with a sigh of regret at the discovery that humanity has not yet emerged from the stage of early childhood. Nazi Germany ostentatiously burns the books it disapproves of, and puts some of their authors into concentration-camps which are the modern equivalent of the pits prepared by the Chinese emperor for the accommodation of the recalcitrant people who refused to be dragooned into acceptance of the new order. The unhappy culprits may or may not live to see the dawn of a German Han dynasty and to rejoice in their recovered freedom of thought and speech ; in any case they have the satisfaction of knowing that not a single one of the condemned books has been or can be annihilated. On the contrary, all of them will doubtless be read more eagerly—perhaps more eagerly than most of them deserve—and will reach a far larger public, than could be hoped for in pre-Nazi Germany ; and libraries and exhibitions containing all the literature that has attracted Nazi hatred will attract pilgrims and readers from all parts of the world.[2]

Unhappily, no such libraries were possible in the days of the " First Emperor " of the Ch'in dynasty in China. The nearest equivalent of such (if we may accept an old tradition) was the famous wall in Confucius's house in which copies of some of the condemned books were concealed during the period of the tyranny and from which they were triumphantly brought out after the accession of the Han dynasty. But though it was impossible to establish libraries of banned books in the China of the third century B.C., there were scholars who somehow escaped with their lives and who constituted themselves into a fraternity similar to the " Society of the Friends of the Library of the Burned Books " which has recently been established in France and England ; and it was due to the efforts of these scholars that a great part, at least, of the condemned books was preserved for posterity.

Ch'in Shih Huang-Ti was but a half-assimilated barbarian, and it need not surprise us that such a man could be guilty of the almost incredible Philistinism—to use no stronger word—of attempting to destroy the ancient culture of China. More disconcerting is it to find that he still carries on a ghostly existence in the China of to-day. There must have been some efficacy in that elixir of life after all ; it seems to have immortalised his spirit, if not his body. There are members of the new Chinese intelligentsia (I apologise for the ugly word) who have not only cut themselves adrift from the old culture and the old morality but have acquired an intense animosity against them, which they are at no pains to conceal in their writings. Some would not only destroy the ethical and spiritual foundations of Chinese culture but would abolish the Chinese language itself, or at least destroy one of the most beautiful productions of the creative mind of man—the Chinese written character. It is only too probable that if they had their way—and doubtless the example of Nazi Germany is a source of encouragement to them—they would have another great bonfire in China, another general destruction of the cultural riches of their country, and that not only would the books in which a great part of those riches is enshrined be given to the flames, but the very language in which they are written. I am not sure that they would shrink from digging a pit for at least 460 rebellious scholars. If they desired to go one better than their spiritual ancestor and patron-saint, the " First Emperor," they might bring the number up to a round five hundred by making the pit large enough to accommodate two score " foreign devils " from England and other countries,

who have had the temerity to plead for the preservation
of all that is beautiful and irreplaceable in Chinese
thought and culture.[3]

I cannot claim originality for the suggestion that the
anti-Confucian crusade of this century has been ani-
mated by the spirit of the " First Emperor."[4] The anti-
Confucian activities of a powerful section of the revolutionary party have been described by many Chinese
as *Chin jih chih fên k'êng*—" the Burning and Burying of
To-day." An article bearing that title was published in
the *Ching Shih Pao*[5]—the Chinese organ of the Confucian Association—in 1923. It contained a letter written by a young Confucian schoolmaster named Chu
Kuang-ming, who wrote out of the fullness of his heart
and from his own bitter experience. He had been brutally
assaulted and imprisoned on false charges because he
had had the courage to continue to teach the Confucian classics after the local educational authorities
had forbidden them to be used in the schools. He
describes, among other things, how a school-inspector
of the new régime had entered his school and was so
infuriated to find the schoolboys reading the classics
that he snatched their books away and burned them.

Although much has happened in the last twenty-two
years to bring something like despair to the hearts of
loyal defenders of the Confucian tradition, the very
parallel between the events of the reign of the " First
Emperor " and those of this era that calls itself republican,
is one which has brought a gleam of hope and encouragement to many. If Confucianism, they say, could survive
one " burning and burying," it can survive another.

For whatever be the true story of the calamity that befell the Confucianism of the third century B.C., it emerged from its dangers and struggles wounded in body but preserving its soul intact. During the centuries that followed, it underwent many changes of fortune, and on several occasions it was forced to yield ground to its Buddhist and Taoist rivals, especially when Buddhism or Taoism happened to be the fashionable cult at the courts of powerful monarchs. But it survived, and went on from century to century, with occasional set-backs but on the whole with added strength and prestige. Setting aside the question of whether Confucianism is a religion or not—a question we have already considered if we have not answered— we may undoubtedly say that for many centuries, and almost up to our own day, it was the predominant State-cult and occupied a position analogous to, if not identical with, that of a national religion.

It has, of course, undergone considerable changes. We of the West used to look upon China as immutable and sunk in a conservatism that was near akin to fossilisation, and Confucianism was held largely responsible for that condition. We were wrong in looking upon China as unchangeable, and we were also wrong in assuming that there was no vitality, no power of growth and adaptation, in Confucianism. Since the Han dynasty, at the beginning of our era, it has often shown the falseness of that assumption. Various modifications in Confucian thought can be distinctly traced to Buddhist and Taoist sources. That remarkable book known as the *Li Yün*, which forms part of the *Li Chi* or " Record of Rites and Ceremonial," and from which I have already quoted, contains material that strikingly exemplifies the Confucian absorption of Taoist ideas. To come down to a much later period, the Confucianism of the Sung dynasty (from the tenth to the thirteenth centuries of our era) underwent a partial transformation at the hands of Confucian scholars who, while often professing to be opponents of Buddhism, had been deeply influenced by Buddhist thought.

It is not my present purpose to describe the changes that Confucianism has undergone in the past as a result of its contact with new ideas emanating from native and foreign sources. I only wish to emphasise the fact that Confucianism is not, and never has been, a closed system impervious to new thought, though it is quite true that bigoted and ultra-conservative scholars have sometimes tried to confine it within their own range of ideas and to give their own interpretations the hallmark of orthodoxy. It is also true that there are characteristics of both Buddhism and Taoism which are definitely of alien texture and to which Confucian thought has always been inflexibly hostile. I need only give as an example the opposition it has consistently shown towards the monastic ideal, or rather to monastic celibacy, and to the adoration of relics. More than 1100 years ago the famous poet and Confucian scholar Han Yü was sentenced to banishment for daring to remonstrate with the emperor for paying superstitious reverence to a " bone of Buddha " brought to China by a pilgrim from India, and true Confucians have always applauded Han Yü for his enlightenment and courage. On the other hand there is much in both Buddhism and Taoism that has been readily assimilated by their more austere rival, and certainly there is nothing whatever in Confucianism that is antagonistic to the scientific spirit or to unfettered enquiry in every department of human thought.

Confucius himself was no blind conservative. *Wên ku erh chih hsin k'o i wei shih i* is a passage which occurs in the canonical *Lun Yü* (" Analects ") and reappears in the *Chung Yung* ("Doctrine of the Mean ").[6] It means that " he who cherishes his old knowledge and is continually acquiring new is fit to be a teacher." Only a few lines further on in the *Chung Yung*, Confucius is made to say that calamity will inevitably befall the man who *while living in the present age is always harking back to the ways of antiquity.* In a footnote to this passage Dr. Legge observes that this " would seem to be a sentiment which should have given course in China to the doctrine of Progress."[7] It was no fault of Confucius that it did not.

Nevertheless, with so many characteristics that should have commended themselves to the modern mind, Confucianism has been going through a period of darkness and peril from which it has not yet emerged. It may be doubted whether during the past eighteen hundred years its fortunes ever fell so low as they fell after the revolution of 1911. There was no intrinsic reason why Confucianism should have suffered danger through the inrush of foreign ideas—political, social, scientific, economic and religious—by which modern China has been inundated ; but its prestige was shattered along with that of the institutions with which it was associated;

it was unjustly made to bear a large share of responsibility for the country's repeated disasters and humiliations ; it was blamed for the failure of the government to uphold the honour of the country in diplomacy and war ; and the muddle-headed conservatism of many of its old-fashioned and reactionary adherents—traitors, as many of them were, to the true Confucian spirit—gave it the appearance of being a stumbling-block in the way of the nation's advancement on modern lines. Above all, it came to be regarded as the strongest bulwark of the monarchy, which in the eyes of the most active and vociferous section of Young China was the irreconcilable enemy of progress and reform.

In the pages of *The Calcutta Review* an astonishing statement was made not long ago by an Indian scholar who in academic circles in India is apparently regarded as an authority on Chinese culture. He informs us that the abolition of the monarchy in China has made no difference to Confucianism and that " the Confucian attitude of mind has not been disturbed in the least."[8]

That such ignorance as this should exist in a country like India, which was at one time, but is unfortunately no longer, in close cultural contact with its great Asiatic neighbour, is disconcerting. No one who had any knowledge of the facts, and who had watched the changes that have taken place in China during the past generation, could possibly make the assertion that the Confucian attitude of mind has " not been disturbed in the least." Not only has it been disturbed ; the disturbance has been profound.

To illustrate the extent to which Confucianism and all

that it stands for have lost prestige in the revolutionary China of to-day, I will narrate three little stories which were told to me many years ago by the great Chinese noble who, as the senior representative of the Confucian clan and descendant of Confucius in the seventy-sixth generation, was the hereditary guardian of his great ancestor's temple and tomb at Ch'ü-Fou. Ch'ü-Fou is a little walled city in south-western Shantung, many of the inhabitants of which have the honour of bearing the surname of the Sage—K'ung—and regard themselves as his lineal descendants. Among other privileges they have the right of burial in the beautifully wooded park in which is to be found the graves of Confucius and of several of his most eminent disciples.

One of the stories told by the Yen Shêng Kung or duke of Extended Sagehood, concerns the famous Chinese rebel and bandit Li Tzŭ-ch'êng. It was this ruffian who was the immediate cause of the collapse of the Ming dynasty and the suicide of the last of the Ming emperors in 1643.⁹ His attempt to found a new dynasty on the ruins of the one he had overthrown was frustrated by the Chinese General Wu San-kuei with the powerful aid of the armies of the young and vigorous empire of Manchuria. This measure quickly resulted in the accession of the Manchu dynasty which, after having produced some of the greatest emperors who have ever ruled in China, was dethroned in 1911.

In the course of his plundering forays, the rebel Li Tzŭ-ch'êng suddenly appeared at the head of his army of robbers before the gates of the sacred city of Ch'ü-Fou, and informed the townsfolk that unless his terms were complied with, he would take the city by storm and slaughter its inhabitants. What he demanded was that the duke should attire himself in his ceremonial robes and put himself at the mercy of the besiegers by mounting the city wall. The duke, against the wishes of many of his friends and fellow-citizens, courageously agreed to comply with the rebel's terms and to sacrifice his own life, if that were necessary, to save his people from slaughter and the temple and tomb of his great ancestor from desecration. Before long the duke of Extended Sagehood, clad in his splendid robes adorned with imperial decorations and insignia of rank, made his appearance on the city wall, above the south gate. He was unattended and unarmed. His weeping and shuddering friends stood in the street below, expecting at any moment to see the duke's body fall to the ground, transfixed by a dozen arrows. For a few moments there was silence. Then the man who had the reputation of being the most brutal, cruel and rapacious of China's many bandit-leaders, emerged on horseback from the front rank of his army and advanced a few paces towards the city-gate. Thereupon he dismounted, bowed to the stately figure on the wall above him, went down on his knees, and prostrated himself in reverent humility. Three times he performed the ceremony of the *kotow* ; then rising to his feet, he once more bowed to the motionless figure still standing on the wall above him, remounted his horse and returned whence he had come. Immediately afterwards the siege was raised, no money-tribute of any kind was demanded from the city or district, and in a few hours' time the bandit-horde had disappeared into the northern mists.

One of the temple officials told me another version of this story which to my mind is much less satisfactory. According to him, the bandit-leader, who surely cannot have been the unmitigated scoundrel Chinese historians have made him out to be, was made the victim of a hoax. The person who appeared on the city wall clad in the robes of the duke of Extended Sagehood was not the duke but someone who was induced to personate him. Nor does this version of the story end there. A few days later, a mysterious sickness seized upon the wretched man who had had the courage to risk his life to save his lord. In spite of his good intentions, he had committed sacrilege by wearing ceremonial robes which did not belong to him and by accepting the homage and reverence due only to the living representative of the Master. Shortly afterwards he paid the penalty of his impiety by death. The other version of the episode is, in my opinion, greatly to be preferred.

The next story for which I have ducal authority is a very similar one. During the T'ai-p'ing rebellion, in the middle of the nineteenth century, a rebel army reached and devastated parts of Shantung. Every village and city made sudden and desperate efforts to defend itself, and numerous mud walls hastily thrown up round peaceful country towns are still standing to testify to the universal panic. In no part of the province was the horror more intense than among the people of Ch'ü-Fou. It was not merely the safety of themselves and their property that they had to look to, but the

I c

preservation of the sacred Temple which heaven had assigned to their safe-keeping. Nothing could ever restore the fortunes of China or of their own proud race —for they were all descendants of Confucius—if the sanctuary should be rifled or destroyed. The imperial armies could render no help, for they had already reeled back in confusion before the victorious on-slaughts of the rebels in another part of the country. A few hundred soldiers was all that the city contained, and they were badly armed and wholly without mili-tary training. The rebels came on, burning and slaying in accordance with their invariable custom. Serious resistance was hopeless and perhaps was hardly con-templated. At last they presented themselves in full battle array before the south gate of the city : the gate that was never opened except to admit an emperor, an imperial envoy, or the duke himself. The majority of the people waited despairingly in their homes for the final catastrophe ; the hardier ones crouched on the ramparts of the city wall and expected to be the first to be cut down in the general massacre. Then a strange sight was witnessed. The serried ranks of the rebel host drew up in a line before the city gate. No shot was fired, no defiant cry reached the anxious ears of the besieged. Then at an unseen signal the whole army went down like one man upon its knees, and every head was bent to the earth in silence. The act of obeisance completed, the host rose up and moved away to the eastward as rapidly and noiselessly as it had come. The greatest danger that had ever threatened the sacred city was averted.

Tomb of CONFUCIUS at Ch'ü-Fou

The last story I have to tell concerns the Sage's tomb. The Chinese say that on one occasion, and on one only, was the grave of Confucius ever in danger of violation. A Mongol invader in the thirteenth century had brought his plundering band of warriors, all as rude and un-cultured as himself, to the neighbourhood of Ch'ü-Fou, and numerous graves of the K'ung family were ruth-lessly broken open and despoiled. At last, when the grave of Confucius himself was about to be desecrated, the leader of the Mongol horde turned to one of the Chinese prisoners captured in the neighbourhood and said, " Whose grave is that ? " " It is the grave of the Master Confucius," was the answer. " Who was Con-fucius ? " demanded the invader. " A philosopher," remarked his prisoner. " A philosopher ! " exclaimed the Mongol. " Then let him rest in peace." Whereupon he cut down and slew with his own hand the luckless warrior who had sought to violate a philosopher's tomb.

Stories of this kind, whether they be authentic or not, illustrate what was till recently a firmly-held popular belief in China, that the home and last resting-place of the great national Sage were under divine protection and could never be desecrated. It was the Chinese belief that even in times of civil war and general up-heaval there was one sacred corner of Chinese soil that would always be treated with reverence.

The popular belief that no hand, however barbarous, would or could be raised against the great Confucian temple at Ch'ü-Fou has been rudely shattered since the revolution of 1911 and the coming of the Republic. The first indication that Ch'ü-Fou was no longer to be treated with reverence followed quickly upon the removal of Confucius from his place of honour as the national Sage. What occurred in 1913 was briefly described by Chang Hsün, who used to be scornfully nicknamed by foreigners and Chinese " the pig-tailed general," and the following extract is taken from my translation of his unpublished autobiography.

" About this time there was an agitation to abolish the cult of Confucius, and people seized the opportunity to begin cutting down the trees [of the Confucian temple at Ch'ü-Fou in Shantung] and carrying off the sacrificial vessels. I immediately despatched troops to protect the holy places, and was just in time to save them from the spoilers. Later on, the Government proposed to take possession of the whole of the sacrificial lands attached to the temple of Confucius and to grant the duke . . . a fixed pension in lieu of his hereditary revenues. This measure was also strenuously opposed by me and it was abandoned. I do not venture to say that this happy result was due to my unaided efforts. I was merely the agent through which the spiritual might of the Sage was manifested."[10]

Unfortunately Chang Hsün was dead, and the Sage found no other agent through whom he could manifest his spiritual might, when a much more lamentable event took place seventeen years later.

In the summer of 1930, during the civil war between the Nanking Government and the rebel armies of "the

Christian General " (Fêng Yü-hsiang) and his temporary ally Yen Hsi-shan of Shansi, the rival forces met in south-western Shantung.[11] Ch'ü-Fou was held by Nanking troops and was attacked by the rebels. No scruples stayed their sacrilegious hands from using modern military weapons against the holy city, and not only the city wall but a portion of the central part of the great temple itself received severe damage. The rebels' allegation was that the Nanking troops had placed and were using machine-guns on the top of the highest building in the city, which was one of the pavilions of the Wên Miao itself—the great Confucian temple—and that they, the besiegers, had used their artillery and other weapons only in self-defence. The allegation was denied by the commander of the Nanking troops, and needless to say, no official enquiry was held to determine the truth. Nor does it make much difference which side was mainly to blame. The facts show that Ch'ü-Fou had lost, perhaps for ever, its privileged position as a sacred city and its immunity from the evils of war ; and that Chinese troops, fighting among themselves, made no effort to protect from damage or desecration the holiest shrine in China.[12]

It may be that July, 1930, marks the nadir of the fortunes of Confucianism. Loyal Confucians—and there are still large numbers of them in China—cannot believe that they will sink lower ; and since that date there have been signs of an upward movement which is perhaps all the better for being slow and gradual. On this subject, more remains to be said.

CHAPTER X

CONFUCIANISM AND THE REVOLUTION OF 1911

FOR SEVERAL DECADES, and especially since the early years of this century, China has been exposed to a torrent of new ideas—political, ethical, social, economic, scientific, artistic, philosophical and religious—which could not fail to have a profoundly disturbing if not a disintegrating effect on the national beliefs and traditions and the whole cultural heritage of the Chinese race. Of that heritage, perhaps the most valuable and apparently the most durable constituent was the Confucian system.

I have already criticised the surprising assertion of an Indian scholar to the effect that recent upheavals in China had made no difference to Confucianism. Had he made this statement a generation ago, when the various reform movements were in their early stages, few would have questioned its accuracy. But it is not true of the China of to-day. Up to the end of the nineteenth century and for several subsequent years, the position of Confucianism was still apparently very strong. Some of the pioneer-reformers—notably the great exponent of the so-called *chin wên* or " Modern Text " school, K'ang Yu-wei—were bold and original commentators on the Confucian canon, but they never wavered in their allegiance to Confucius or in their recognition of him as the father of Chinese civilisation.[1]

In pre-revolutionary days the chief opponents of Confucianism were foreigners, or Chinese who had come under foreign influences. Christian missionaries were far from unanimous in their estimates of Confucianism as a rule of life, and they differed among themselves as to whether it could rightly be called a religion ; but most of them saw in it a serious obstacle to the spread of the Christian faith. They felt that Buddhism and Taoism were decaying forces which they could afford to disregard ; and with regard to modern Taoism, at least, they were doubtless right. But Confucianism with its undeniably lofty code of morals, its relative freedom from superstitious accretions, and its high prestige among all classes of the Chinese people, presented a much graver problem.[2]

The subject of the attitude of the Christian missionaries in China towards Confucianism is a very delicate one to handle when one is addressing a Christian audience, to the majority of whom the cause of the evangelisation of the " heathen " is by far the most sublime of all causes to which the energies of Christendom can be devoted. In a frank discussion of the subject, the risk of giving offence is very great, and had it been possible to avoid the topic altogether I should have been glad to do so. But the Christian contribution to the forces which have to a great extent undermined the Confucian position has been far too great to be ignored.

Many Christian missionaries, both Catholic and Protestant, have been industrious and successful students of the Confucian classics, but the fact that they were primarily Christian evangelists and only secondarily students of Chinese literature has left its unmistakable marks on their translations and commentaries. Such marks are very numerous in the writings of the great sinologue, Dr. J. Legge. For example, in a note on a passage in the canonical *Shu Ching* he expresses the desire that some Christian scholar would produce, for the benefit of Chinese readers, a commentary which would " clearly and minutely " unfold " the errors on the constitution of nature and the course of providence of which it is full." He adds : " From this ground we might go on to shake the stronghold of their confidence in all the ancient teachings and the wisdom of their so-called sages."[3]

In their efforts to shake the confidence of the Chinese people " in all the ancient teachings " and in " the wisdom of their so-called sages," the Christian evangelists were actuated only by the most exalted motives ; moreover they were firmly convinced that they were able to offer the Chinese people a substitute for the ancient teachings which would far more than compensate for their loss. Their critical attitude towards the Confucian traditions had very little effect on the Chinese people as a whole or on the Confucian *literati* as a class, but they achieved considerable success among their own converts and those whom they could influence through their schools. Their task was simplified by the fact that the vast majority of their converts belonged to the unlettered classes who did not feel called upon, and certainly were not qualified, to act as the champions of the national traditions.

The not unnatural hope and expectation of the missionaries was that the ground lost by Confucianism would be won and occupied by Christianity. No blame attaches to them for not having foreseen that a great part, at least, of the ground would be occupied by the forces of atheism, materialism and communism. But their optimistic enthusiasm should not have led them to the hasty assumption that a non-Confucian China would necessarily be a Christian China or that the Chinese people would derive moral or spiritual benefit from the overthrow of the Confucian system. Many of the wiser missionaries now recognise that they and their predecessors were grievously mistaken in this matter, and contemplate the possibility of a revival of Confucianism with sympathetic interest and almost with approval.

Before the overthrow of the monarchy, Christian missionaries were in the habit of repudiating with indignation the accusation often made in official Confucian circles that Chinese Christians were tainted with revolutionary tendencies or with disloyalty to the Throne. On frequent occasions they rashly declared that their converts were among " the best and most loyal " of Chinese subjects.[4] In 1907 there was held at Shanghai a Centenary Missionary Conference at which were passed several very sensible resolutions intended to emphasise the " wholly moral and spiritual aims " of Protestant missionaries in China. In one of these

resolutions the Conference recommended all missionaries "to be vigilant, lest, in the present national
awakening, the Christian Church should in any way
be made use of for revolutionary ends, and lest Chinese
Christians should, through ignorance, confusion of
thought, or misdirected zeal, be led into acts of disloyalty against the Government."

The very fact that it was thought necessary to give
expression to this recommendation seems to indicate
that the missionary societies were vaguely conscious
that some of the Christian organisations were being
utilised for purposes that scarcely deserved the description of " moral and spiritual " ; though in a subsequent
" resolution " they endeavoured to banish their suspicions in this matter by stating that " we teach and
enjoin on all converts the duty of loyalty to the powers
that be," and by stoutly affirming " that in fact there
are no more loyal subjects of the Empire than the
Chinese Christians." The Edinburgh Conference of
1910 accepted this statement as correct, for it laid
emphasis on the fact that " missionaries of all Societies
. . . insist upon the paramount duty of respect for
Government," and states that " the Christian community, though often discouraged and sometimes per-
secuted, is *the most law-abiding and loyal* section of the
community."[5]

The Manchu Government, in spite of all its faults and
shortcomings, knew a good deal more about the aims
and aspirations of certain sections of its subjects than
the missionary societies gave it credit for, and it certainly far excelled the missionaries in its knowledge of

the Chinese character and its comprehension of Chinese motives. It had strong reason to suspect that many of the Christian converts were by no means so well-disposed towards the reigning dynasty or towards the existing political constitution as the foreign missionary body professed to believe ; and yet it knew only too well from bitter experience that if it made any serious attempt to bring them to punishment or to exercise supervision or control over the Christian societies to which they belonged, the missionary body would immediately accuse it of persecuting innocent Christians and of breaking its solemn treaties with the armed Powers of the West.

It soon became plain to all the world that the Manchu Government was right in its suspicions and that the missionaries were wrong. The missionaries assured us in 1910 that the Christian faith as taught in China successfully inculcated " loyalty to the throne."[6] The following year saw the outbreak of a revolution which had several Chinese Christians and " enquirers " among its most prominent leaders, many of whom had deliberately made use of Christian organisations for the furtherance of revolutionary aims. There were members of the missionary body, and sympathisers with missionary work, who subsequently (after the success of the revolution) admitted that such was the case, and who agreed with the Rev. C. S. Medhurst, of Shanghai, in his statement that " the initiator of the Chinese Revolution was the Christian missionary."[7] From all parts of the country, at the outbreak of the Revolution, came the news that among the Christians of China were to be found members of the " extreme left " of the revolutionary party. An English naval chaplain, writing to me from the Fuhkien province a month after the outbreak of civil war, informed me that his ship had been visited by numbers of educated Chinese, including a party of Christians connected with a local missionary institution. " All of them," he said, " were red-hot revolutionaries."

It would of course be unjustifiable to assert that the Christians of China had no right to co-operate with their non-Christian fellow-countrymen in patriotic activities or in any movements directed towards the amelioration of the deplorable social and political conditions of their country. Many of us may have our doubts as to whether the desired reforms (which, nearly a quarter of a century after the revolution, are still far from accomplishment) could not have been brought about by a more satisfactory and less costly process than by revolution. We cannot ignore the fact that the principle of constitutional government had already been accepted by the Manchu Court and that preparations were actually in progress, when the revolution broke out, for the summoning of a parliament which was to have met for the first time during the year 1913. The revolutionaries, however, were convinced that as a preliminary to the inauguration of a Golden Age of progress and prosperity the Manchu oligarchy must be removed and the imperial throne demolished. Whether they were right or wrong, it is a fact that some of the revolutionary leaders were men of ability and patriotism, and it would be absurd to contend that Chinese Christians had not as much right as Chinese Confucians or Chinese Buddhists to join the ranks of those who believed in revolution as the panacea for the woes of China.

But while we admit this to the full, we cannot ignore the undeniable fact that the missionaries were wrong in their repeated assertions that the influence of the Christian propaganda was wholly spiritual and moral, that Christian converts were noted for their exceptional loyalty to the Throne, and that the Christian churches were wholly free from any association with political agitation or intrigue. The true state of affairs was concisely stated by a well-informed correspondent of *The Times* who, in April 1913, drew attention to the fact that in many parts of China the cause of Christianity was identified in the public mind with the cause of the uprising against the dynasty. "Many of the revolutionary leaders," he wrote, "were Christians. Many revolutionists who were not Christians *attended the churches in the months before the great rebellion and used them to spread their ideas*. The missionaries stopped this as far as they could, but the movement was too strong for them. The younger Church members, their minds influenced by Western ideas, *became in place after place, leaders of revolt*."[8]

One missionary journal (the organ of the Seventh Day Adventists) actually went so far as to admit to its columns an article in which the people of China were advised to rise in rebellion. This was a few months before the outbreak of the revolution. The fact that the foreign members of the Mission in question professed ignorance of the contents of the article (which was in the Chinese language) and agreed, when it was brought to their notice, to withdraw the number from circulation, only serves to show that foreign missionaries in China were liable to become the unconscious instruments of political agitators.

There is no reason to doubt the good faith of the missionaries who declared that they had tried hard to prevent their churches from becoming the channels of revolutionary agitation, but there is ample ground for the belief that they were not always scrupulously careful to follow the recommendation made at the Edinburgh Conference of 1910 that missionaries should "keep clear of all party and faction."[9] It was admitted in the Report of the Conference that some missionaries had "not been sufficiently regardful of national sentiment *or of the duty of upholding loyalty to the imperial government,*"[10] and it was definitely laid down that "missionaries should have nothing to do with political agitation. This is outside their sphere, and engaging in it can only harm their work. . . . The relation of the missionary, as such, to the convert is purely religious. He has to him no peculiar civil relation which in the least entitles him to interfere in the general administration of the country."[11]

Whatever may be said of the attitude of the Christian Churches and their Chinese converts towards the monarchy and other established institutions of China in the years immediately preceding 1911, there is no doubt that they eagerly welcomed the revolution when it came and were willing enough to accept credit for having brought it about.[12] It is not surprising, then, that on the establishment of a so-called republic the missionary bodies in China looked forward to a new era of expansion for the Christian evangel and that some of the more sanguine missionaries even foresaw the early conversion of " China's millions " to the Christian Faith.

Christians in China—both Chinese and foreign— were quick to make the most of their enhanced prestige. It was obvious that the Manchu dynasty had forfeited the " divine decree " (*T'ien-ming*) and that Heaven was on the side of the revolutionaries. But the Christians were on the side of the revolutionaries too, therefore the missionaries could not have been in error when they declared that the work on which they were engaged had been entrusted to them by God. The Christians stood for Western civilisation and material progress, so did the republicans. It was the aim of the Christians to overthrow Buddhism and Taoism, and to supersede Confucianism except in so far as its ethics could be engrafted on or merged in those of Christianity. The republicans too—or an " advanced " and militant section of them—were only too ready to pour scorn on the religious and ethical systems that had satisfied their forefathers, and, though not necessarily attracted by the dogmas of the Christian faith, they transcended the highest hopes of many of their missionary allies in their headlong eagerness to incorporate their social and political dreams and visions in a fantastic edifice to be built of foreign materials amid the ruins of the venerable fabric of Chinese culture.

This being so, it is not surprising that in 1913 an event took place which created a much greater sensation throughout European and American Christendom than it did in China itself. The new republican government took the hitherto unheard-of step of asking for Christian prayers on behalf of the infant republic.

There is no question but that the official favours bestowed on Christians and on Christianity after the dethronement of the Manchus were largely due to considerations of political expediency. The new government of China, not yet firmly seated in its place of power, was naturally anxious to gain friendship and official recognition from Western governments, and it well knew there was no simpler or more effective means of winning the support of certain powerful and influential sections of the European and American peoples, and incidentally of obtaining ready access to Western money-markets, than by paying public respect to the Christian religion.

By no means is it suggested that by adopting such tactics as inviting Christians throughout China and the world to set aside a day for public prayers on behalf of the infant republic of China, the responsible members of the government were one and all actuated by considerations of statecraft. There were and are many sincere Christians in China (those who assert that no " real " conversions ever take place among the Chinese are in error), and there is reason to believe that the famous appeal for Christian prayer was prompted by a perfectly genuine religious conviction on the part of a certain prominent member of the Chinese Cabinet who at that time held the portfolio of Minister of Foreign Affairs. This was Mr. Lu Chêng-hsiang, a devout Catholic who has since found his spiritual home within the walls of a Catholic monastery in Europe. Yet it would be a mistake to ignore the fact that the appeal for the prayers of Christendom issued from a Cabinet which acted entirely on its own responsibility and soon passed out of existence. Contrary to a prevalent notion in the West, the suggestion did not emanate from the newly-summoned representative Houses, nor was it in accordance with any known wish of the Chinese people, all but a minute fraction of whom never knew anything about it.[13]

The unexpected action taken by the Cabinet on this occasion synchronised with a serious crisis in the financial and political affairs of the nation, and it may be suggested without cynicism that some, at least, of the members of the Cabinet who assented to the suggestion of an appeal for a Day of Prayer were actuated by a variety of motives among which the spiritual motive was not supreme. It is a significant fact that in the official message in which the request for prayers was embodied, special mention was made of the desirability of a speedy recognition of the Chinese republic by the foreign Powers. A special correspondent of *The Times* pointed out in connection with this subject that "the sympathy of Christian peoples is expected to take a practical form by their admitting China to her rightful place in the family of civilised nations and by conceding to the people equality of treatment in matters of trade and emigration."[14]

Kα

The exultation produced in Christian circles in China by the episode of " Prayer Sunday " and other indications of official leanings towards Christianity expressed itself in various manifestations which many people who were by no means ill-disposed toward Christianity thought regrettable. One group of Christians, taking advantage of the fact that the overthrow of the monarchy had caused the suspension of certain religious solemnities which from time immemorial had been conducted by the emperor, took temporary possession of the beautiful and most sacred Altar of Heaven, where they proceeded to hold Christian services and to sing Christian hymns. The patriotism and the religious sentiments of many non-Christian Chinese were shocked by an act which in their eyes was blasphemous or at least highly indecorous, and a similar view was taken by many foreigners in China, who knew that the sacrificial rites hitherto conducted by the Chinese emperor, in his capacity of Son of Heaven and Father of his people, had been associated with a system of worship which had constituted the religious background of Chinese life for unnumbered centuries.[15]

Equally significant of the growth of a spirit of arrogance among Chinese Christians was the conduct of certain highly-placed officers of the government, who, having become converts to Christianity, tried to make use of their official position to propagate the tenets of their new creed and to overthrow the ancestral faiths of their fellow-countrymen. One of these was a Christian Chinese named Chung Jung-kuang, who was appointed by the republican government to the important post of Director of Education in the Canton province. The position was one which afforded ample scope for the activities of a religious zealot ; and Mr. Chung acted in accordance with the expectations of his fellow-Christians. His crusade against Confucianism speedily evoked an outburst of resentment and indignation among the educated Cantonese who still retained some reverence for the religious and ethical ideals and traditions of their race. Numerous strongly-worded telegrams and memorials were addressed to the central government protesting against the proceedings of Chung Jung-kuang. It would be erroneous to suppose that the memorialists belonged to a reactionary section of elderly scholars who were actuated by a spirit of bigoted conservatism and were out of touch with modern intellectual and religious movements. Among them were many who had taken a zealous part in the revolution and had been honourably associated for many years in schemes for political and social reform ; and some of the most emphatic protests against the attempt to abolish the Confucian cult came from a group of influential Chinese merchants resident in the British Colony of Hong-kong.[16] The agitation, as we shall see, bore fruit in due season, and resulted in Chung Jung-kuang's disappearance from the official world of republican China.

In another part of the country a great commotion was caused by the conduct of certain Christian officials who allowed themselves to be so far carried away by religious zeal that they imposed taxation on the people of their districts for the express purpose of financing their own schemes for the propagation of Christianity. Perhaps their supporters might have attempted to justify their action on the ground that they were only turning the tables on the officials of the old régime, who had applied a portion of the proceeds of taxation to the maintenance of the Confucian or Buddhist cults. But the fallacy of the argument is obvious when we remember that Confucianism was a long-established State-cult and that Buddhism was a religion which was professed by many tens of millions of the Chinese people. Christianity, on the other hand, was professed by no more than a fraction of one per cent of the population, it still required the fostering aid of thousands of foreign missionaries and vast sums of foreign money, and still showed no disposition, at that time, to surrender the rights and privileges secured to it by what afterwards came to be known as " the unequal treaties." Such being the case, we cannot be surprised that the arbitrary proceedings of these Christian officials were instrumental in creating a situation which, in one district at least, was admitted by foreign missionaries to be one of " acute difficulty."[17]

CHAPTER XI

CONFUCIANISM AND THE REPUBLIC

ALTHOUGH Christian missionaries in China were largely responsible for the lowered prestige of Confucius during the revolutionary period and encouraged " Young China " in its belief that the doctrines of the Sage were outworn and incompatible with republican institutions, there were a few wise and experienced missionaries who took no part in the anti-Confucian movement and watched its progress with deep misgivings. One of these was the Rev. John Ross of Manchuria, one of the most venerated missionaries of his day. Writing in a periodical called *China*, published by the Christian Literature Society, in the year following the establishment of the republic, he warned his readers that " those who slight Confucianism appear to have neglected to weigh its influence on the past of China, or its probable place in its future. Missionaries are usually so much occupied with the numerous details of their daily work that they have little leisure to devote to a thorough study of the spirit and full meaning of the Confucian system. Yet all that is good in the China of to-day is the product of this system." He went on to say that not a few earnest missionaries had made enemies of the Confucian Chinese because in speaking of Confucius they had " displayed ignorance of his teaching and misrepresented his beliefs. *There is in Confucianism nothing incompatible with the progress, social, political or spiritual, of the Chinese people.* The missionary should claim him as an ally, not oppose him as a foe."[1]

A little later, another highly respected missionary in China—archdeacon A. E. Moule—wrote as follows :

> " It is difficult to believe that the attempt recently made by some ardent spirits of Young China to discredit and banish from their curriculum of education the writings of Confucius and Mencius, as out of accord with republican principles, can succeed, save with grave discredit cast upon Chinese intelligence and most justifiable *amour-propre.*"[2]

Before Dr. Moule's book had passed through the printers' hands the pendulum had begun to swing back and a reversal of the anti-Confucian policy that had marked the early days of the republic had already been set in motion. In a footnote he adds these words : " As these pages pass through the press, civil war has broken out. . . . Among some symptoms that some check is to be placed on headlong change may be noted the quite recent restoration of the worship of Confucius in the schools and colleges."[3]

As might have been expected, the anti-Confucian agitators had over-reached themselves in their revolutionary zeal, and the first of a series of conservative reactions had become visible as early as 1913. The very government which had gladdened the hearts of Christians throughout the world by calling upon them to offer up Christian prayers for the welfare of the Chinese State, a few months later issued stern edicts against the demolition or neglect of Confucian temples and invited the governors of all the provinces to consult with the central authorities as to the best means of preserving Confucian principles in politics and social life and of safeguarding the cult of " our most holy Sage." We have seen that a Christian Director of Education had found himself strong enough to set public opinion at defiance by banishing the Confucian cult from the institutions under his control ; but by a presidential mandate issued on August 25th, 1913, that same official was summarily " ordered to vacate his post."⁴ A little later, the newly-founded Confucian Association, which found strong support in every province, announced that the solemn rites associated with the Confucian cult would be publicly performed in Peking on the morning of September 3rd. No statement had previously been made as to whether the solemnities were to be held under government patronage or not ; yet they were graced by the presence of a large number of the highest officials in the State. One of these was the representative of the president himself, on whose behalf a long and impressive speech was made on the importance of maintaining Confucianism as the basis of the national culture. Confucian ceremonies on a still more imposing scale were held during the same month at the great Confucian temple in the city of Ch'ü-Fou.

Simultaneously with these proceedings, the Education Department at Peking was diligently employed in drawing up new school text-books which embodied the moral teachings of the Confucian School ; and the governments of the various provinces were urged, and indeed commanded, to make the Confucian classics the basis of the national education.

This reaction in favour of Confucianism was undoubtedly to a very great extent popular throughout the country. It was admitted by a missionary organ which was far from pro-Confucian in its attitude that " on the occasion of the recent anniversary of the birthday of Confucius, the reactionary temper of the people was shown by great rejoicings and demonstrations in certain centres."[5] But the reaction would never have gone as far as it did without the active approval of the president. Yüan Shih-k'ai, in his inaugural address, on October 10th, 1913, " confessed his devotion to the old traditions of his country," and declared that " the immortal traditions and precepts " of Confucianism " must not be lightly swept into oblivion." They had always, he said, been for China " a great moral support," and he was convinced that the chances and changes of four thousand years had " left the essence of the doctrine secure from the ravages of time." He censored those who were " deluded by theory " and who were ready lightly to abandon their own cultural heritage.[6]

Shortly afterwards, towards the end of November, Yüan Shih-k'ai issued a presidential mandate inculcating the duty of doing reverence to Confucius. The following is an extract from the English translation which appeared in the foreign press in China early in December, 1913.

" The moral teaching of Confucius is like the sun and moon shining in heaven and the rivers flowing on earth. It stands as the guide to preceptors for myriads of years, being always new through hundreds of generations. Whosoever has blood and breath gratefully acknowledges his indebtedness to the sage teachings of Confucius which are perfectly good and with which nothing can compare. Throughout our history for over two thousand years the moral teachings of Confucius have always been followed and he has been held in reverence as the most holy Sage. During the creation of our new nation, he should be shown still higher honour and respect. . . . The exalted ideal held before us by Confucius is comparable with a lofty mountain : the longer we gaze, the more we admire."[7]

In the same mandate the president referred to a recent ceremonial visit paid to him by K'ung Ling-yi, the *Yen Shêng Kung* or Duke of Extended Sagehood, and announced that the honours conferred under various imperial dynasties upon the senior living descendant and representative of the Sage would continue to be recognised under the republic, and that the ritual observances connected with the Confucian cult would also be maintained.

There is no reason to doubt the sincerity of Yüan

Shih-k'ai's homage to Confucius and his teachings, but Yüan himself was distrusted—with very good reason—both by monarchists and by republicans, and his patronage did the cause of Confucianism more harm than good.[8] In his hands, the Confucian system was merely a political instrument. He hoped by its aid to pave his way to the Throne, and there is no doubt that the use he made of it tended to discredit Confucianism in republican circles and to strengthen the belief that the Confucian system and the institution of monarchy rose or fell together. The radical Ch'ên Tu-hsiu, afterwards an active communist, was a strenuous supporter of this view, and his influence over the young intellectuals of his time was very great.[9] Moreover, by such actions as throwing the well-known scholar Chang T'ai-yen into prison for expressing unorthodox views on the interpretation of the Confucian canon, Yüan Shih-k'ai played into the hands of those who held that Confucianism was opposed to liberty of thought.[10]

Meanwhile the reaction in favour of Confucianism and the old traditions was regarded with something like dismay by many members of the missionary bodies in China. To quote an editorial Note in one of their organs, " the elation of the past is now giving way to apprehension."[11] Another missionary periodical referred with regret to " the revival of the ancient sacrifices to Heaven and of the more modern worship of Confucius."[12] But on the same page it notes that " the decadence of Chinese ideals in the sphere of morality " had been " a deplorable feature of recent conditions " and threatened " to destroy that fair fame for honesty and straightness which Chinese traders have so deservedly enjoyed." This was a candid and significant admission, for it is an acknowledged fact that " the decadence of Chinese ideals in the sphere of morality " synchronised with the growing disregard for the old Confucian teachings and standards.

It is interesting to find, even at this early stage, the beginnings of a suspicion, in the minds of well-informed missionaries, that Sun Yat-sen was not the great philosopher and sage statesman that China needed for her political and moral salvation. The fact that he was a baptised Christian had naturally been a source of pride and gratification to the Protestant churches at the time of the revolution ; yet as early as the third year of the republic some of his missionary friends were already speaking of his " lack of balance of mind " which had " long been obvious except to the colourblind."[13] In later years, when the political party of which he had been the acknowledged leader became the dominant factor in Chinese politics, adverse opinions of this kind were discreetly left unspoken.

The Confucian reaction associated with the presidency of Yüan Shih-k'ai (1913–1916) was referred to in the following terms by a correspondent of a prominent London newspaper.

" By re-establishing the worship of Heaven and the sacrifices to Confucius he [Yüan Shih-k'ai] is to all intents and purposes constituting a State religion, and the decision is certain to be severely criticized.

The truth is that reaction is paramount and, as usual in China, is even more violent than the reform movement which preceded it. The latest act of the president is a significant commentary on the intercessions called for last year by the Government from the Christian churches throughout the world on behalf of the young Republic."[14]

The last sentence, which refers of course to the episode of " Prayer Sunday " already described, seems to reveal a curious attitude of mind. Apparently it was right and fitting that the Chinese Government should specially ask for Christian prayer, but the same non-Christian Government was guilty of " violent reaction " when it accorded official recognition to religious or quasi-religious observances which had been a part of the ceremonial life of China for hundreds or thousands of years. It was a matter for rejoicing that Christian hymns should have been sung at the Altar of Heaven, but a matter for regret that the head of the Chinese State should exercise what had been the sacred prerogative of the Chinese sovereigns for unnumbered centuries by offering up on that white marble Altar the ceremonial sacrifices which constituted the very purpose of its existence.[15]

The statement of the English journalist that by re-establishing the worship of Heaven (in other words the worship of God) and the sacrifices to Confucius the Chinese Government was to all intents and purposes establishing a State religion brings us to a very important episode in that long struggle which throughout the past quarter of a century has been carried on between various contending forces for the rich prize of the Soul of China.

Allusion has already been made to a movement aimed at the recognition of Confucianism as the State-religion or State-cult of China, and I pointed out that the motive underlying the movement was not a desire to raise Confucius from the rank of human sagehood to that of godhead, but the belief that unless the cult were given the status of a religion, and its position guaranteed by the constitution, it would be handi-capped in its struggle against its rivals.[16]

The Confucian Association, which came into existence as soon as the whirlpool of the revolution seemed likely to engulf all that was held sacred by those who clung to the old traditions, was founded by a group of scholars among whom the leading spirit was Ch'ên Huan-chang, a Cantonese disciple of the great scholar and reformer K'ang Yu-wei. Though steeped in the traditional learning, this Confucian enthusiast was familiar with Western culture, he had taken his doctorate in an American university, and he had written in English a valuable work entitled *The Economic Principles of Confucius and his School*.[17] Besides taking a leading part in the activities of the Associa-ton (which he preferred to call a " Church ") he became editor of an excellent Confucian periodical named *Ching Shih Pao*, to which most of the foremost Confucian scholars in China were frequent and regular contributors.

The principal objects which Dr. Ch'ên Huan-chang

and his colleagues had in view were two. In the first place they strove for the insertion of a clause in the republican constitution whereby Confucianism should be recognised as the religion of the State ; in the second place they aimed at the retention of Confucian ethics as the basis of the national system of education, and especially at the foundation of Confucian universities. The first of the universities were to be at Peking and Ch'ü-Fou—Peking because it was the cultural and political capital of China, Ch'ü-Fou because of its historical associations with the Sage himself.

With regard to the University scheme, there is little to be said. No Confucian university has yet arisen either at Peking or at Ch'ü-Fou. A site for the Peking university was acquired and the foundations for a great building were prepared at considerable cost, but before any further progress could be made, the growing political chaos in the country and the anti-Confucian policy of the Kuomintang caused the whole scheme to be shelved. Nevertheless Confucian schools were established both in Peking and in Ch'ü-Fou, and periodical gatherings of the Confucian Association and its numerous branches were held at these and many other centres and did much to remind the people of China that the cause of Confucianism was not yet dead. I attended some of the Peking meetings in the company of Dr. Ch'ên Huang-chang, and had the pleasure of listening to eloquent addresses by many Confucian scholars of whom perhaps the most distinguished was the venerable Ma Ch'i-ch'ang.[18] On one such occasion the gathering was addressed in Chinese by Dr. Richard

Wilhelm, the well-known German scholar, whose recent death was a sad blow to sinology.[19]

The question of giving formal recognition to Confucianism through the written constitution was one which was hotly debated in China's ramshackle parliament for several years. In 1913 a parliamentary committee was appointed to prepare a draft of the permanent constitution which was to take the place of the provisional constitution adopted on the establishment of the republic. In September of that year one of its members presented a memorandum in which the State-recognition of Confucianism was strongly advocated, and the question soon became a burning one both in parliament and in the country. When it was brought before parliament, on the first division there were 255 votes in favour of the proposal, 264 against. It was therefore defeated by the narrow margin of 9 votes. But that did not settle the matter, for the question was reopened on several occasions and was still a living one as late as 1923.

The first public indication that the Christians were taking alarm was contained in a letter addressed to the leading English newspaper in China by a Peking correspondent who declared himself to be actuated by " an earnest desire for the welfare and growth of Christianity in China " and by the fear that if Confucianism or any other religion were introduced into the constitution the growth of Christianity would be " greatly curbed."[20] He went on to say that " by early concerted action we Christians may be able to stop the movement," and that he and other Christians had already elected a committee of seven whose duty it would be to devise measures for carrying on a counter-campaign against those who sought "to associate religion with politics" by recognising Confucianism as the State cult. The protest was strongly supported in the editorial columns ; but while throwing the weight of its influence on the side of the discontented Christians, the newspaper in question was scrupulously respectful in its references to Confucianism. On one point only could its comments be described as unfair or misleading. It stated that if the efforts of the Confucians were to succeed, the services of "some of the best men in China "—Christians—" would inevitably be lost to the State."

In these words we have a reference to the oft-repeated allegation that under the old régime no conscientious Chinese Christian could become an official as he would be obliged to do violence to his religious principles by taking part in ceremonies of a non-Christian character. This was one of the complaints which came up for discussion at the Edinburgh Missionary Conference of 1910, and which had to be withdrawn from the records of the Conference in consequence of the vigorous protests of an outspoken Chinese Christian named Dr. C. C. Wang.[21] Christian converts had not been debarred from becoming Government officials under the Manchu dynasty ; and the supporters of the proposal to make Confucianism the State cult under the republic were emphatic in their assurances that there was no intention to exclude them from office, or to impose conditions which they would be unable to accept. They declared that no Christian official would be required or expected to take part in Confucian ceremonies if he had a conscientious objection to so doing. Complete freedom of religious belief and practice was to be guaranteed by the constitution itself to all citizens of the republic, including Government officials ; and active participation in Confucian rites would not be required from non-Confucians.

These assurances did not satisfy the Christians. In September 1913, a Protestant missionary (Mr. E. W. Thwing) gave a lecture in which he declared that to make Confucianism the State religion " would be a grave mistake, as it would be repudiating, in a measure, the religious liberty guaranteed by the Provisional Constitution. It would be interfering with one of the most sacred rights of the citizens of this nation, the right of personal choice as to religious belief."

In a letter which was published in the *Peking Daily News* of September 24th I commented on Mr. Thwing's statement in the following terms :

" It is not only by Mr. Thwing that this argument has been brought forward. It is being strongly emphasised by every writer or speaker, Chinese or foreign, who is opposed to the important proposal now under the consideration of the Constitution Committee. It is apparently realised by them that the most effective method of defeating the proposal is to inspire the Chinese people with the fear that to declare Confucianism the State religion would be to inflict a deadly blow on the principle of religious liberty.

L c

"I am in a position to assure your readers that there is not the slightest wish or intention on the part of the Confucian party to interfere in the smallest degree with the religious beliefs or practices of any of the Chinese people. The supporters of Confucianism have made it perfectly clear in their public utterances that they have no desire whatever to oppose or show hostility to other religions.

"There is an Established Church in England and another in Scotland, yet an Englishman or a Scotsman is perfectly free to belong to any Church he pleases, or to no Church. Religious liberty is guaranteed to the Englishman just as effectively as it is guaranteed to the American, in spite of the fact that in England there is a State Church whereas in the United States there is none."[22]

The attitude of the Christians towards the proposal to make Confucianism the State cult was resented very bitterly in Confucian circles, mainly for two reasons. In the first place, it was felt that the question was one for the Chinese people to decide for themselves, without foreign interference. Christians of all denominations in China numbered less than one *per cent* of the population, and the Christian Churches derived most of their strength from foreign sources. The Confucians were perhaps not wholly unreasonable when they questioned whether a religious organisation which was foreign in origin, which still looked mainly to the West for its means of support, and which was largely amenable to Western control and influence, was justified in taking an active part in the settlement of a constitutional and religious question which was, after all, the concern of the people of China.

In the second place the Confucians resented the Christian attitude because they had had ample experience of what seemed to them to be Christian arrogance and intolerance, and they felt that if the numerical positions of Christians and Confucians were reversed, the Christians would speedily forget their arguments against the principle of a State religion and would have no hesitation in seeking special privileges for their own faith. The Confucians, rightly or wrongly, doubted the sincerity of the Christians when they asserted that the existence of a State religion was incompatible with religious liberty, and they suspected that the Christian hostility to the Confucian proposal was based on something like jealousy. The Christians knew that so long as they themselves numbered but a small fraction of the population, they could not hope to induce the Government to declare Christianity the State religion, but they were determined to do their utmost to prevent any rival religion or cult from enjoying the prestige which the status of an established religion would confer.

Had it not been for the atmosphere of suspicion and hostility created by the missionary bodies in China, it is improbable that there would have been any widespread opposition to the proposed establishment of Confucianism as the State cult, except among China's " bright young men " who rebelled on principle against all that was authoritative and traditional.[23] The Confucians themselves held, with much justice, that there would be no innovation in declaring Confucianism to be the State cult. It had been so for something like two thousand years. The insertion of the proposed clause in the new written constitution would merely give constitutional sanction to an existing well-recognised fact. It might even be argued that not only Confucianism but also Buddhism and Taoism were State cults or Established Churches, for all had enjoyed imperial patronage and support. If it be replied that the term *kuo chiao* (national teaching, religion or cult) had not been in use, and that no imperial Edict had ever been issued specifically declaring Confucianism or any of its rivals to be the State cult or National Religion, it may be pointed out that the position of Confucianism in China was, in that respect, not very different from that of Christianity in England. No one denies the fact of the existence of an Established Church in England, yet the " Establishment " has never been defined by law. " There is no single Act of Parliament," as Walter Hobhouse has reminded us, " by which the Church was ever ' established,' as by some Napoleonic concordat ; for in England the Church is, in a true sense, older than the State."[24] The same writer quotes a well-known authority on Church Law : " The ' establishment' of the Church has been effected in reality by its gradual assimilation with our national life, and not by Act of Parliament."[25]

It is equally true to say of Confucianism that in the course of its long history—much longer than that of Christianity in England—it underwent a " gradual assimilation with the national life." In that sense

Tomb of MENCIUS at Tsou-Hsien, Shantung

Confucianism was an Established Cult or Religion (it matters little which term we prefer) many centuries before there was any idea of defining its status in the republican constitution.[26]

This was clearly recognised by several of the ablest Chinese Confucians who took part in the constitutional controversy. One of them pointed out that the vitality of the Chinese race was undoubtedly due in great measure to the teachings of Confucius, and that for long ages the Confucian doctrines had been the staple food on which the mind of China had been fed. Confucianism had " long been recognised," he said, " as the State religion of China." That being so, what could be more appropriate than to give it a place of honour in the permanent constitution ? " This action is simply to turn the unwritten law, which has been in force for two thousand years, into a written law."

This writer's article closed with the emphatic pronouncement that " Confucianism is the most important characteristic of the Chinese nation, from which the national spirit of our people derives its inspiration. If it is allowed to go into oblivion, the standard of morality will become lower day by day, and there will be nothing in the country to inspire the people to maintain their ancient civilisation."[27]

These last words may be regarded as a key to the real problem that faced the constitution-builders of the new China. The question as to whether China should have a State religion or not was subordinate to the much more important question whether the national civilisation was to be built up anew on a Western basis, or whether its foundations were to remain Chinese. To quote the same Confucian writer again, " What we wish to impress upon the people is that any independent country should have some distinguishing characteristics all its own in regard to arts, science, culture, and religion, which will tend to strengthen the vitality of the country."[28]

Large numbers of those Chinese who looked with favour on the proposal to give Confucianism the constitutional status of a State religion did so not necessarily because they approved of established Churches on principle, but because they knew that Confucianism had for ages been intimately associated with the history, civilisation and life of the Chinese race, because they held that the people of China had the right to expect this fact to receive full recognition in the written constitution of the new Republic, and because they believed that unless this recognition were accorded, China would be in grave danger of becoming a disinherited mendicant among the nations of the world.

" The moral patrimony of every individual cannot be sought for elsewhere than in the native soil which has given birth to himself or to his ancestors." These words were published just a year before the outbreak of the Great War. They were written not by a Chinese but by a European, who was concerned, not with the civilisation of China but with what was described as the revival of the moral vigour of the French people—a revival which the writer unhesitatingly attributed, in very large measure, to a growing tendency to

" re-establish the Catholic traditions of France." It was admitted that the reawakening among Frenchmen of an interest in religion did not necessarily indicate a recrudescence of faith in doubtful or discarded dogmas, but was largely based on a patriotic belief that " the greatness of a nation "—to quote the writer's words— " depends on its cultivating and developing its specific national traits ; and that the development of such traits, consequently the development of the specific genius of the race, of all that which can alone make the race great, is impossible—nay, unthinkable—unless the individual remain constantly in close touch with the native soil. . . . A nation cut adrift from its traditions is like a ship without a compass in unknown and stormy seas. Bereft of its traditions, of the rules of conduct established by the experience of countless generations, a nation is necessarily a prey to anarchy ; reduced to such a condition, society can have no hold over its component individuals, can furnish the latter with no adequate principle of action." [29]

Now it is an amazing fact that while Europeans are ready enough to admit the adequacy of such arguments as these when Christianity and the races of Christendom are concerned, they are extremely unwilling to acknowledge the relevancy of the same arguments when applied to the circumstances of an Oriental race or to a religion or ethical system that is not of Christian origin.[30] Europe and America have sent hundreds and thousands of missionaries to China, many of whom have used their best efforts to convince the Chinese that the doctrines of the ancient sages of China are characterised by " absurdity, insufficiency and sinfulness "[31] ; that such virtues as patriotism are impossible unless the Chinese change their religion[32] ; that Confucianism is responsible for the various calamities which have befallen China during the past century[33] ; and that the Confucian system has no candle to light men on their way through life.[34] Among China's Western advisers there have been many who have contemplated with satisfaction the tendency of an influential section of Young China to break away from the traditions— social, political and religious—of their race and country ; who are filled with rejoicing when they hear that some village elders have banned the teaching of the Confucian classics in their schools[35] ; who assure the Chinese people, with a confidence born of ignorance, that " the whole philosophy of Confucius is upset "[36] ; and who with equanimity declare of Confucian literature that " its strength is spent " and that it " savours of death."[37] It is fortunate indeed that there have always been missionaries who have taken a fairer and more generous view of Confucianism than those who in their perhaps misdirected zeal have uttered these and similar judgments. Dr. John Ross of Manchuria, quoted at the beginning of this chapter, was one of these ; and he has had numerous successors who in educational and other spheres are doing excellent work in China to-day and who are broad-minded and enlightened enough to do what Dr. Ross rightly declared all missionaries should do—claim Confucius as an ally, not oppose him as a foe.

The Chinese and foreign opponents of the proposal to

make Confucianism part of the constitutional law of the land were victorious over the Confucian party, but their victory proved, after all, to be a barren one. Incessant strife between rival parliaments, bitter feuds between the various groups of politicians each of which claimed the right to speak for the people of China, made it impossible for any one political party to frame a constitution that had any chance of meeting with general acceptance. It is true that a so-called constitution was somewhat hastily put together in time for the inauguration of Ts'ao K'un as president in 1923, but neither Ts'ao K'un nor his constitution was recognised by the Cantonese party, and the document which was solemnly promulgated at Peking, and officially communicated to the diplomatic body, became a dead letter as soon as the " Christian General " and his confederates had seized the supreme power in Peking towards the end of 1924 and had forcibly ejected Ts'ao K'un from the presidential chair.

Six years ago, when the anti-Confucian movement under the auspices of the Cantonese party and the Kuomintang was approaching its zenith, the Minister of Education under the " Southern " government at Nanking issued circular instructions to all educational institutions under Kuomintang control in which the official attitude towards Confucianism was made very clear. The customary spring and autumn sacrifices were to be discontinued, all Confucian temples were to be converted into schools and their revenues diverted to purely educational uses, and the teaching of the Confucian classics in universities and colleges was peremptorily forbidden. The cabinet minister who was responsible for these instructions was Ts'ai Yüan-p'ei, formerly chancellor of the Peking National University. For several years he had been one of the guiding spirits of " Young China," and he had distinguished himself as an " advanced " teacher in politics, economics, literature, and other spheres of intellectual activity. Unlike Chung Jung-kuang, who, as we have seen, had tried in the early days of revolutionary fervour to substitute Christianity for Confucianism, and to do it by forcible means, Ts'ai Yüan-p'ei was not actuated by any pro-Christian sympathies. On the contrary, he was a resolute and outspoken adversary of every form of religion, and was the leader of a movement to substitute the fine arts for religion as an outlet for the activities of the human spirit.[38] The anti-Confucian polemic of Ts'ai Yüan-p'ei was therefore not regarded in missionary circles as in any way advantageous to the Christian evangel.

Ts'ai Yüan-p'ei's ministerial proceedings, supported as they were by the Kuomintang cabinet to which he belonged, aroused deep indignation in Confucian circles, and the utterances of various leaders of public opinion in China made it clear that if Ts'ai Yüan-p'ei could claim to be the accredited spokesman of the Nanking authorities, he was not entitled to speak for the people of China. Ex-president Li Yüan-hung, the nominal leader of the military revolt against the Manchus in 1911, had already expressed his regret that the young men of the present day lacked an ethical education on Confucian lines, and " emphasised that the future education of China must be in accordance with Confucian ethics."

The decrees of the Kuomintang and of Ts'ai Yüan-p'ei carried no weight in northern China at that time, and at the very moment when the abolition of the study of the classics was being decreed in central and southern China, the provincial authorities in Tientsin were making that study compulsory. " The Tientsin district magistrate and the chairman of the Chihli provincial assembly have been ordered to make an inspection of the various schools and to report if there is any case where this order is not obeyed."[39] Simultaneously, the northern administration at Peking, then under the control of marshal Chang Tso-lin, issued decrees appointing the ministers of Home Affairs and of Education to be the principal participants in the approaching spring ceremonies of the Confucian cult ; and all local officials were " ordered to make full preparations in accordance with the rites formerly observed by the Manchu court." Moreover, all government schools and colleges, with the exception of primary schools, " were ordered to make the study of the Confucian classics compulsory."[40]

The collapse of the northern administration, the death of Chang Tso-lin, and the removal of the capital from Peking (thenceforth to be known as Peiping, one of the old names of the northern city before it became the capital) to Nanking, gave the victory, for the time being, to the anti-Confucian party.

Throughout the greater part of China, never did the prospects of Confucianism seem more gloomy than they were during the seven dismal years that followed 1923—the period of the modern counterpart of " the Burning of the Books and the Burial of the Scholars." During those years many incidents occurred that filled the hearts not only of loyal Confucian Chinese but also of many foreign friends of China with disgust if not with despair. At Hankow, early in 1927, a portrait of Confucius was torn down and deliberately trampled underfoot ; and an English speaker at the annual meeting of the China Association held in London on April 24th asked—after reporting and commenting upon this incident—" what was the use of making agreements with people who did that sort of thing ? "[41] Three years later the rival armies of north and south met and fought one another in the " holy land " of Confucianism, and showed far less reverence for the great temple of the national Sage than had been shown by the most ruthless of the rebel hordes that devastated half China in the seventeenth and nineteenth centuries. I have already indicated that year—1930—as the year in which Confucianism may be said to have touched the nadir of its fortunes.[42]

CHAPTER XII

CONFUCIANISM AND THE CHINA OF TO-MORROW

THOSE CHINESE who, through all the hazards and changes of the past three decades of turmoil and revolution, have remained loyal to the Confucian tradition, hope and believe that the period of the second " Burning and Burying " has come to an end. On the whole it may be said that there are good grounds for a moderate optimism. From many parts of China we hear of a growing anxiety for a return to the old Confucian teachings and standards in the spheres of morality and conduct. It is not only among the conservatives and " reactionaries " that this anxiety is visible ; it now exists even among the left-wing radicals and among people who cannot for a moment be suspected of hankering after a return to the *ancien régime* in the sphere of politics. Thus it is that in many parts of China there are clear signs of something like a Confucian revival.[1]

Perhaps the most significant feature of this revival is the fact that it is occurring simultaneously in northern, southern and western China. Even in Canton, the home of the Kuomintang and the headquarters of many revolutionary movements in ancient and modern times, it is increasing in strength and popularity. Ch'ên Chi-t'ang, the Governor of the province, is in active sympathy with the movement and has made " Back to the Classics " a slogan that is echoed in every part of the Canton province.[2] It is heard in the mercantile circles of the provincial capital (and therefore also in commercial Hong-Kong) and it has been taken up by influential groups of Cantonese university students.

Describing the movement towards the end of 1932, a foreign observer declared that it was locally regarded " as a means to check the moral deterioration of the present generation, and to realise national salvation." He continued as follows :

" Supporters of the campaign hold the steady disappearance of the old virtues as taught by the ' Pattern of 10,000 generations ' [Confucius] accountable for all the existing political and social chaos as well as the present national crisis. They maintain that had the Confucian teachings not been neglected, China would not be in the state she is in to-day.

" On the occasion of the birthday of Confucius, which occurred only recently, impressive ceremonies were held at which a glowing tribute was paid to the great Sage. . . .

" In pre-Republican days Confucianism had a firm footing in Canton, the Confucian ideals of life and conduct permeating the whole people. Even to-day, notwithstanding the spirit of revolution and the abolition of Confucian worship, the influence of the Sage still lives on. On the occasion of his birthday not only educational institutions held celebrations, but all the business people joined in the observances. Possibly Canton is the only city where on Confucius's birthday all shops and stores remain closed and a general holiday is declared. The tremendous enthusiasm with which the event has been celebrated every year can hardly be equalled in any other city.

" Supporters of the ' revive-the-old-culture ' movement maintain that the virtues Confucius extolled are virtues in great need of being popularised to-day, and have even suggested that the study of Confucianism should be made, like the study of Sun-Yat-senism, compulsory in schools and colleges. Upholding the Confucian teachings, a Chinese journal in Canton comments : ' Show us any system of philosophy comparable to that of Confucius which for well nigh two thousand and five hundred years has swayed the morals of the people of a great nation. This is truly unchallengeable ! ' "[3]

Under the conditions that have prevailed in China during the past twenty years, there is very little harmony or similarity in outlook between one province and another. Yet even from the far-western province of Ssŭ-ch'uan we hear of a new impetus being given to the old learning that many people thought had been for ever discarded. Of Tachienlu, a town of mixed Tibetan and Chinese population, we are told that " one outstanding feature of the year's work [in the schools] was the prominence given to the Chinese classics. The two early morning hours, from seven till nine a.m., were given exclusively to the classics." Very significant is the fact that this renewed interest in the Confucian teachings was fostered by the local French Catholic Mission, by which an important public school is conducted and financed. The actual teaching is carried on by a Chinese principal aided by twelve Chinese and Tibetan teachers. But it is not the only centre of Confucian studies in Tachienlu. "The Chinese classics are now taught in several schools," and in Tachienlu it is hoped " that the Four Books, with their high ethical teaching and moral implications, will not be relegated to what may be termed ' the good old-fashioned days.' In these books the love of rightness and friendship and chastity and justice are carefully and faithfully inculcated, and it would be a great pity to see this teaching disregarded and ignored." The European correspondent from whom this information is derived adds that in the country schools of the district might still be found the old-time Chinese dominie, " who loves to dwell on the old classical literature of China, and sees the only hope for a dark and uncertain future in a return to the ethical teaching of China's sages."[4]

The revival of Confucianism, if at this early stage we may venture to use this expression, is not confined to the territory under the real or nominal control of the republican government. At the beginning of these lectures I referred to the determined and successful effort made by the Chinese colonists in Java about twenty-five years ago to ensure that their children should not be deprived of their Confucian birthright.

This was not a unique instance of the survival of an interest in Confucian teaching among overseas Chinese, nor was it by any means the last. There is an active Confucian Association to-day among the Chinese of the Straits Settlements and Malaya, and a short manifesto issued by them in the spring of 1933 is of special interest, especially when we remember that practically all the Chinese of Malaya come from southern China, including the Kuangtung (Canton) and Fuhkien provinces, and that no section of the Chinese people has been more exposed than the Malayan Chinese to the impact of Western and other alien ideas of the kind most likely to bring about the disruption of the cultural traditions of their race.

The manifesto is too long to be quoted in full, but the following is a rough abstract and translation of its opening paragraphs.

" The ancient system which has been the ethical stronghold of the Chinese people during the last two thousand years has been crumbling before the surging waves of new ideas—good and bad—which are simultaneously finding their way into the minds not only of the student-class but of all sections of our people.

" Among the so-called *mo-têng* (modern) Chinese there is a marked absence of the sagacity requisite to a proper appreciation of the ethical philosophy and teachings of Confucius, and a lack of zeal for truth and justice, industry, self-denial, moderation and public duty.

" Only the future will show how far the teachings

Mc

of Confucius will survive among the people of our country both at home and abroad, and thereby enable them to co-operate with the peoples of other countries in leading humanity safely to that elevated plane to which the lofty ideals of our Sage aimed at leading us. Not yet has the Western world, for all its wisdom, appreciated the profound forces for good that are embodied in the teachings of our Sage."

The past few months have witnessed the beginnings of a new movement in China which may conceivably retard the progress of the Confucian revival but which may also find in Confucianism the ethical and spiritual basis which it must have if its influence is to be permanent. I refer to the *Hsin Shêng-huo Yün-tung*—" the New Life Movement "—which was officially inaugurated by marshal Chiang Chieh-shih (Chiang Kai-shek) early in 1934, and has since spread very rapidly through all parts of the country including provinces over which the authority of the Nanking government is, at the best, shadowy. It is a movement directed towards the improvement of public and private morals and the inculcation of public spirit, frugality, good manners, fidelity, honesty and zeal in the performance of duties, modesty and truth, cleanliness, self-discipline.

According to a published report, the movement originated in an accidental encounter between the marshal and a Chinese student whom he observed quarrelling and fighting on the street, with a cigarette in his mouth. The sight distressed him so much that the idea of organising a movement for the regeneration of public life and conduct forthwith took root in his mind.[5] His first speech on the subject was made at Nan-ch'ang, the capital of the province of Kiangsi in February, 1934.

From the ethical standpoint the spiritual kinship of the new movement with Confucianism was recognised at the outset, for marshal Chiang exhorted his audience to return to the old Confucian virtues of *Li, I, Lien, Ch'ih*, which may be said to denote courtesy and good manners, justice and uprightness, frugality and integrity, modesty and self-respect ; and although no attempt appears to have been made, as yet, specifically to associate the movement with any existing religion or cult, its natural affiliation would certainly be with the Confucian system.

By April, 1934, the ideas underlying the movement had caught the public imagination to such an extent that mass-meetings and lantern-processions in favour of the " New Life " were being held in many of the greatest cities in China, from Canton in the south to Peiping in the north, and large sums of money were being subscribed for the creation of a building in Nan-ch'ang which was to become the headquarters of the movement and the radiating centre of its numerous activities. In connection with a lantern-procession at I-chang it was reported that one school had a huge lantern in the shape of a coffin, in which had been placed symbols of all the bad customs which it was the business of the New Life to eradicate, such as opium-smoking, wine-drinking, gambling and other forms of immorality ; and attached to the head of the coffin

was a paper reproduction of a gravestone on which was
written the date of burial.[6]

Dr. Chu Chia-hua, a leading educational authority,
spoke of the movement as one " for the regeneration of
our race " and as " a response to the urgent demand
of the whole nation as well as a manifestation of the
spirit of the age." He described it further in an article
published in an English newspaper in Shanghai.

> " It has as its basis the time-honoured [Con-
> fucian] virtues of propriety, justice, integrity and the
> sense of shame, is animated by the spirit of the race
> as revealed in history, and aims at the broadening
> and deepening of that spirit. It starts with the daily
> life of the individual and culminates in the har-
> monious development of all his faculties ; it begins
> with the improvement of the individual life and ends
> in the development of the life of the nation."

This, of course, is pure Confucianism as we find it
in such canonical books as the *Ta Hsüeh* and *Chung
Yung*. Dr. Chu Chia-hua goes on to criticise very
frankly the degeneration that he sees around him.

> " Politeness and courtesy are gone, order and dis-
> cipline have disappeared, and the sense of respon-
> sibility is a virtue conspicuously rare. Flourishing
> like noxious plants are corruption, confusion and the
> sense of futility and world-weariness. . . . Ever since
> the Boxer uprising, the Chinese race has entirely
> lost faith in its own destiny. While many reform
> movements were started . . . they were nothing more

than attempts at mechanical imitation of the ex-
ternals of foreign countries, resulting in the complete
submergence of the real spirit of the Chinese people
as revealed in its history. All the policies and systems
of foreign countries were seized upon as a panacea
for the social and political maladies of China, without any attempt being made to find out whether
they were adapted to the conditions of this country.
Anarchism, communism, internationalism and other
' isms ' made confusion worse confounded and
brought about the collapse of our own system and
the destruction of our own cultural heritage. What
is worse, the youths of that generation, tumbled out
of this seething cauldron, sowed the seeds of future
disaster and thus diminished the vitality of the
nation. . . . Marshal Chiang's purpose in starting the
New Life Movement is to remould the whole social
fabric with a view to carrying out all kinds of reforms
and to developing the education of the Chinese
people with all the force and power possessed by
Chinese society as a whole. We should therefore
push forward the New Life Movement in accordance with that purpose, and we should realise at the
same time that this movement must start with the
education of young men by training them to form
the habits required by the New Life."[7]

If it must still be regarded as an open question
whether the New Life Movement will or will not
affiliate itself with Confucianism, in spite of its whole-
hearted endorsement of what we may call the

Confucian virtues and the Confucian attitude towards
the major problems of human life, we can entertain
no such doubts concerning another movement which
since 1932 has been a dominant factor in the political
and social evolution of a large and important part of
what was known to the Western world, not quite
accurately, as the Chinese Empire.[8]

I refer to the movement directed at the realisation,
in the new Manchuria, of the old Confucian conception of *Wang Tao*—the "Royal Road" or "The
King's Highway."

Ancient as this conception is in Confucian thought,
the Western world heard little of it until it made a
modest and rather mysterious appearance in the pages
of what is known as the Lytton Report—that is to say
the report issued by the Commissioners appointed by
the League of Nations to investigate the situation in
Manchuria.

" The aim of the government," says the Report, " is
to rule in accordance with the fundamental principle
of ' Wang Tao.' It is difficult to find an exact English
equivalent for this phrase . . . which may have many
shades of meaning."[9]

Certainly the term is capable of various interpretations. But it does not require deep research into Chinese
literature to arrive at a fairly accurate idea of what it
meant and still means in the political philosophy of
Confucianism.

One of the sections of that venerable Chinese classic,
the *Shu Ching*—the canonical book of early Chinese
history, of varying degrees of authenticity—contains a

rhymed ballad which in all probability is much older than the prose text in which it is embedded. It is to be found in that part of the classic which is known as *Hung Fan* or " The Great Pattern." It is put into the mouth of a great noble who had been asked by king Wu, founder of the Chou dynasty (more than a thousand years B.C.), for advice on the subject of true kingly rule. After a lengthy discourse on the art of government, the noble quotes the old ballad, of which the following is a rough translation.

> *Free from bias, free from prejudice,*
> *Follow the Royal Way of righteousness.*
> *Turn not to right or left,*
> *But follow the King's Highway.*
> *Free from hatred,*
> *Follow the Royal Road,*
> *With no leanings to person or party.*
>
> *Broad and long is the King's Highway.*
> *With no leanings to party or person,*
> *Tread the smooth surface of the Royal Way.*
> *Free from turnings or deviations*
> *The King's Highway is true and straight.*
> *Behold its perfection and thereby be guided.*

Having recited the poem, the noble adds the following exhortation.

" These words are an announcement of the transcendent excellence of the Royal Way, which has a law and a lesson that come from God. All the people of the realm, having learned the lesson and the law and having set themselves to be guided thereby, will draw near to the glory of the Son of Heaven and hail him as their father and as their sovereign lord."

" Son of Heaven " is, of course, one of the earliest titles given to the Emperor, and was meant to signify that he held a divine commission (*T'ien-ming*) to rule his people—a commission which might be, and often was, withdrawn from an unworthy ruler.

This mystical teaching of the *Wang Tao* or Royal Road is repeated and restated in many of the later books that enshrine the Confucian philosophy. It appears, for example, in the *Book of Mencius*, though it is there spoken of as *Wang Chêng* or " True Royal Government." In one passage we read that " in the State of Sung true royal government is not practised. If it were, all the peoples within the four seas "—that is, all the inhabitants of the known world—" would be lifting up their heads longing for the coming of the prince of Sung to be their ruler."[10]

The Confucian theory was that the expansion of a State by force of arms was not only wrong but useless when the ruler was one who governed according to the principles of *Wang Tao* or *Wang Chêng*. Surrounding peoples or potential enemies would be conquered, or rather absorbed, not by violence or militarism but by justice, magnanimity and the peaceful and orderly development of the arts of civilised life. There was no need for the ideal Chinese ruler to " break the heathen " in his endeavour to " uphold the right." The " heathen " would come of their own accord and kneel before him, or await his coming with longing anxiety. It might occasionally be necessary to castigate evil rulers who oppressed their subjects or who trampled the principles of Wang Tao underfoot, but their peoples must be treated with generosity and magnanimity.

The theory is illustrated in another passage of *The Book of Mencius*, which I translate as follows :

" The expedition against Ko was the first of eleven punitive expeditions undertaken by T'ang, yet in the whole empire he had not a single enemy. When he warred in the east, the western tribes murmured jealously ; when he fought in the south, the northern tribes felt aggrieved. ' Why ' they cried ' does he leave us to the last ? ' The people longed for him just as they long for rain in a time of drought. And his activities never interfered with their marketings or obliged them to cease their labours in the fields. It was only the bad rulers that he sought to destroy. To their subjects he came as a sympathetic friend. To them his coming was indeed a cause of joy, like a fall of seasonable rain."[11]

Not the most credulous can believe that these conditions were ever fully realised or that the many wars waged in ancient and modern China have invariably been " righteous." Doubtless in ancient China as in modern Europe all wars were " righteous " from the point of view of those who took up arms. Nevertheless the lofty Confucian ideal has been an inspiration to generations of China's leaders of thought and action and has helped to mould the characters of many of her greatest rulers and heroes.

I have already quoted several times from that delightful thesaurus of Chinese political wisdom, the *Shuo Yüan* of Liu Hsiang. There is a passage in that work in which " three forms of government " are named and described.

" There is the *wang-chê chih chêng*—' the royal way of government '—which is government by *hua*, the peaceful transformation of the people by a benign evolution, [mainly effected by the good example set by sage rulers] ; the government of the dictator (*pa*) who rules by his own authority and prestige and by keeping the people in awe of him ; and the government of the despot, who rules by force."[12]

These three forms of government are compared, and the place of honour is, of course, reserved for the first.

The man who is chiefly responsible for the establishment of the principle of *Wang Tao* as the ideal to be aimed at (though he himself would be the first to admit that it has not yet been realised) by the government of the new Manchurian Empire, is no other than that great Confucian scholar, poet and statesman to whom I referred at the beginning of these lectures and who drew up the " Fourteen Confucian Texts " there translated and explained. Long before the new Empire was inaugurated, and during the years of poverty and obscurity which his loyalty to his emperor imposed upon him, Chêng Hsiao-hsü often spoke to me of the dearest ambition of his life—to be in a position in which he could take a share in the building-up of a system of government founded on the Confucian principles of *Wang Tao*. Rightly or wrongly, he believes that in the evening of his life the longed-for opportunity has come.

I have already quoted the brief and rather cryptic reference to *Wang Tao* made in the Lytton Report. On another page of the same document we are told that after the former emperor of China, whose reign-style had been Hsüan-T'ung, had been invited to become Chief Executive (*Chih Chêng*) of Manchuria, it was decided that " the new era of government was to be styled " Tatung " (Great Harmony)."[13]

Nothing is said of the reason for the adoption of the style "Tatung." (This phrase, according to the system of transliteration generally used by English-speaking scholars, should be written Ta T'ung.) The members of the League of Nations Commission were apparently left in ignorance of the intimate connection between that style and the *Wang Tao* ideal of government.

To find that connection we must turn to the *Li Yün*, one of the books comprised in the canonical *Li Chi* or " Record of Rites and Ceremonial " from which I have already quoted. In eloquent language we are told in that book how the following of the principles of *Wang Tao* or the Royal Way will lead to the final establishment of Ta T'ung—" the Grand Harmony," or, as the phrase has been justifiably translated, " World Brother-hood."

In the passage of which I am about to offer a rendering we read of the happy condition of a State in which

the king and his ministers act in accordance with the
principles of the *Ta Tao* or " Great Way "—here used
for *Wang Tao*.

" Under these blissful conditions, the Empire
existed for the good of the people. Virtuous and
able men were chosen as rulers, men who cultivated
sincerity of speech and kindliness in their relations
with all. The people, in extending their loving
devotion to their own families, were not forgetful of
the interests of others. Maintenance was provided for
the aged to the end of their lives, employment for the
able-bodied, nurture for the young. Tender care was
given to the widowed, the orphaned, the childless, the
sick. The right of men to the work that suited them,
and of women to good homes, was recognised. The
production of goods was so regulated that nothing
was wasted, while useless accumulations for private
use were regarded with disapproval.[14] Labour was
so regulated that energy was stimulated, while
activity for merely selfish reasons was discouraged.
Thus there was no room for the development of a
narrow egoism. Robbery and outrage were unknown,
hence there was no shutting of outer gates. Such was
the age of *Ta T'ung*—' World Brotherhood.' "[15]

The picture here given us is of course that of another
never-realised ideal. It is only the Utopia of a Chinese
sage who in Plato might have found a spiritual brother.
Yet who will deny that it deserves our admiration?
The passage, and others like it, seem to suggest that

there is very little in the programmes of our own social reformers that would astonish a Confucian philosopher of the Han dynasty were he to be re-born in twentieth-century Europe. The germs of our social service legislation are readily traceable in the literature with which he was familiar. It would seem that the Confucian age and that which succeeded it were confronted with social and economic problems closely analogous to those that confront us to-day ; and indeed from other sources we know that such was indeed the case.

Wang Tao is now being taught and expounded in all Manchurian schools and colleges, and a society (the *Wang Tao Hsüeh Hui*) exists for the purpose of spreading a knowledge of it among the people. The first number of the society's admirable Chinese periodical (which contains articles in colloquial as well as literary Chinese and will therefore have a popular appeal) is named *Wang Tao Ts'ung K'an*, and the first number was published at Mukden on March 20th of " the first year of K'ang Tê "—namely, 1934.[16] Contributors to it included Chêng Hsiao-hsü himself, and the noted scholars Ch'êng K'o-hsiang and Chêng T'ai-i.

A perusal of the articles contained in this periodical should convince all who can read Chinese of the absurdity of the suggestion (which has been made in an ill-informed section of the press) that the Wang Tao doctrine was inspired or imposed on Manchuria by Japan. Inasmuch as Wang Tao is essentially anti-nationalistic and anti-militaristic, it seems hardly likely that Japan, which is rightly or wrongly credited in Europe and America with being the embodiment of

extreme nationalism and militarism, would encourage
the growth of ideas of world-brotherhood and universal
peace which, once accepted in Manchuria, might
easily spread to Japan. It is indeed a significant
fact that the principles of Wang Tao have already
begun to influence Japanese political thought to an
extent which some of Japan's military leaders may find
embarrassing. Some recent remarks on this subject by
a Japanese writer, Mr. Toshio Shiratori, are worth
quoting.

" As all efforts are bent in Manchuria to the
creation of a state where the Confucian ' Kingly
Way ' may prevail and where there may be no
exploitation of man by man, so in Japan a return to
the ' Way of the Tenno ' (the Heavenly Ruler) and
the eradication of all the baneful aspects of the
materialistic civilisation are impetuously demanded.
Thus the Manchurian affair must be regarded only
as a sort of prelude to the real movement."[17]

Another more pardonable misconception about
Wang Tao is that its very name (the " Kingly Way ")
stamps it as essentially anti-democratic, and that it is
applicable only to a State ruled by a benevolent despot.
Such a view completely ignores the fact that China's
model sage-kings, who are supposed to have exempli-
fied the working of the principles of Wang Tao in the
highest degree, are believed to have risen from the
ranks of the common people and to have been life-
presidents rather than monarchs. The hereditary

Official Announcement of the Confucian principles of Wang Tao on which the new Government of Manchuria proposes to be based. The calligraphy is that of the famous Confucian scholar and statesman Chêng Hsiao-hsü, and the Announcement was issued in the name of the present Emperor of Manchuria, former Emperor of China, on the occasion of the proclamation of the new State in 1932.

principle had not been established, and the ruler was chosen simply for his fitness to rule. The doctrine of the *T'ien-ming* or " divine decree," which was frequently withdrawn from an unworthy and bestowed upon a worthy ruler, is a similar indication that the Chinese kingship was in theory elective.[18]

In the English Coronation Service, a Bible is handed to the newly enthroned monarch with the words " This is the Royal Law, these are the lively oracles of God." In a very similar sense, *Wang Tao* is, for Confucian China, the " Royal Law."

As Wang Tao does not necessarily imply a monarchical form of government, there is no intrinsic reason why Manchuria should have a monopoly of it. The philosophy of Wang Tao is part of the cultural inheritance of the Chinese race and is not the private property of that section of it which inhabits the region north of the Great Wall. Nevertheless it is hardly to be expected, in the peculiar circumstances of the present time, that Chinese republicans will readily adopt " Wang Tao " as their political slogan or as the guiding principle of their polity. In their own *Hsin Shêng-huo* or " New Life " movement, however, they possess what ought to be an adequate substitute for Wang Tao, unless, like so many other promising movements in modern China, it is doomed to an early death. The New Life movement has, indeed, one advantage over Wang Tao, in that the latter is, to a large extent, a code to be followed by the ruling classes for the good of the governed, and may therefore be regarded as aristocratic, whereas the New Life is essentially a popular movement. The fact that it was initiated by a prominent leader of the Nanking Government is immaterial. The very rapidity with which it has spread throughout China shows that it awakened an immediate popular response, and suggest that the Chinese people were themselves consciously or subconsciously aware of those defects in the " Old Life " which made the " New Life " an imperative necessity.

But there need be no conflict between *Wang Tao* and *Hsin Shêng-huo*. They both aim at the happiness, the regeneration and the moral and material welfare of the people. Both are in agreement with traditional Confucian principles and are therefore in complete harmony with one another. They also transcend national boundaries and bring a wholesome lesson to all mankind.

" *When the schemes and all the systems, Kingdoms and Republics fall,*
Something kindlier, higher, holier—all for each and each for all."

Tennyson, we may assume, had never heard of *Wang Tao* ; yet he taught one of its essential doctrines in these two lines of *Locksley Hall*.

Politically, as all the world knows, Manchuria and China are sundered by a chasm—or a Great Wall. Spiritually they are brethren, and will remain so. Much might be said in confirmation of this bold statement, but perhaps for our present purpose it is needless to do more than put side by side the following items of news—one from Manchuria, the other from China.

Mukden, Manchuria,
September 3rd, 1933.

In view of the fact that the new State of Manchuria has made the doctrine of Confucianism the standard of national morality, Confucius Day, which fell to-day, was celebrated with grand fête throughout the country. In Hsin-king, the capital, the grand cere-mony was held in the Confucian shrine with the attendance of premier Chêng and other high officials of the Government. Mean-while, the fête was observed practically all over the country. The Banks, Government offices, schools and other public institu-tions declared a holiday to-day.

Shanghai,
June 4th, 1934.

The birthday of Confucius has been included in the list of na-tional holidays in China. This decision was adopted by the Central Executive Committee of the Kuomintang that held a meeting on June 1st, presided over by Sun Fo [son of Sun Yat-sen], chairman of the Legislative Coun-cil, Nanking. The observance of Confucius's birthday as a Chinese national holiday is significant. The Tri-People principle of the late Dr. Sun Yat-sen has been propagated throughout the country at the expense of Confu-cianism, which was the exclusive guiding spirit of Chinese moral principles. Importance is attached to the motive of the Kuomintang in reviving and supporting Con-fucianism.

The violence of the attacks launched against Con-fucianism by left-wing revolutionaries and by radicals whose spiritual home was Moscow or anywhere except China, have tended to create a belief that the Kuo-mintang is officially committed to an anti-Confucian policy and that there can be no real revival of Con-fucianism under the present system of government. But in spite of the undeniably true statement made in the above-quoted report from Shanghai that Dr. Sun's principles had been propagated at the expense of Confucianism, we have only to turn to the pages of the

Nc

San-Min Chu-i of Dr. Sun to see that he himself was no enemy of Confucianism. Dr. Sun, though estranged from much that is characteristic in Chinese culture, insisted on the necessity of a return to the old Chinese morality and strongly recommended his countrymen to retain all that was good in Confucian philosophy. He even commended the principles of *Wang Tao*, though one of his translators, fearing that a literal translation might suggest a betrayal of republican principles, is careful to render the phrase not by the term " Kingly Way " but by " The Way of Right."[19]

It is also worthy of note that one of the ablest and most respected members of the Kuomintang Government—Mr. Tai Chi-t'ao—has written a valuable Chinese work (well worthy of translation into English) entitled " The Foundations of the Philosophy of the San-Min Principles of Sun Wên " (*Sun Wên Chu-i chih chê-hsüeh ti Chi-ch'u*). His book is a learned and spirited defence of his belief that those " foundations " are Confucian.[20]

But if Confucianism is not only to survive but is also to make a valuable contribution to the great work of national reconstruction which is the most urgent task confronting the Chinese people at the present day, it is essential that it should be a Confucianism that will adapt itself to new needs and prove itself capable of dealing with new problems. I have already pointed out the error of supposing that there has been no vitality, no power of growth and adaptation in Confucianism during past ages, and there is no good reason to suppose that it possesses these qualities no longer.

In 1923 I was invited by the Confucian Society of Tsing Hua University, near Peking, to address it on the subject of the prospects of Confucianism in China, and in the course of my address I spoke these words.

" One result of the anti-Confucian movement which, at least to a foreigner, seems almost wholly good, is that it has forced Confucians to consider, more seriously than they ever did before, the claims of Chinese philosophers outside the charmed circle of Confucian orthodoxy, to the recognition and fame hitherto denied them by the orthodox schools. For example, it is no longer legitimate, if it ever was so, to condemn Mo Ti or Yang Chu merely on the ground that they were condemned by Mencius. Their teachings must be judged on their merits, so far as mutilated texts allow, and if praise or dispraise is to be meted out to either or both, it must be on some ground that can be defended against the attacks of opponents whom the mere weight of orthodox Confucian opinion would wholly fail to impress. . . .

" As the members of this Society are all young and are being educated on Western lines in a progressive modern University in China, I hope I may safely assume that the spirit of critical enquiry which you are encouraged to cultivate in other branches of learning will not desert you when you are studying the Confucian classics." [21]

Confucianism, as I have already remarked, has not disdained to borrow from other systems, such as

Buddhism and Taoism. A very striking example of how Taoist ideas have been absorbed by Confucianism is to be found in the famous passage quoted above in which we are told of the age of Grand Harmony or World Brotherhood. Many orthodox Confucians have admitted, a little unwillingly perhaps in some cases, that the words which in that passage are ascribed to Confucius himself not only were never uttered by the Sage but, like other parts of the *Li Yün*, have a distinctly Taoist flavour.[22] Sometimes this intrusion of Taoist or Buddhist ideas into Confucian literature is referred to as if it were something to be ashamed of, or as if Confucianism had been detected in the act of petty plagiarism. But the very fact that Taoist teachings could be so harmonised with Confucian orthodoxy as to find an accepted place in a Confucian classic is in itself a striking illustration of the truth that Confucianism had the property shared by all living organisms—that of assimilation and absorption. Just as Christianity possessed and exercised the right and the power to assimilate the philosophy of the Neoplatonists, so Confucianism possessed the right and power to assimilate what it found good in alien systems. Assuredly it must continue to exercise the same privileges if it is to live and thrive in the new China.

What loyal Confucians must do, if they wish their Master to remain what he has been for two thousand years, the Sage and supreme Teacher of the Chinese people, is to act on the advice recently given to the followers of a very different teacher—Karl Marx. They

must " disentangle in his teaching, from what is dead
or no longer appropriate, what remains alive and
capable of that growth and adaptation which is the
prerogative of living things."[23]

Confucianism, I maintain, is a living thing, and I
doubt whether there is anything in the Confucian
teachings that is really dead. But if there is, it must be
ruthlessly excised and cast away.

Confucianism has the right to be regarded as the
philosophia perennis or " Great Tradition " of the Chinese
race, in the sense in which Dr. W. R. Inge applies
those terms to the Christian-Aristotelian-Neoplatonic
tradition in Europe.[24] This right will not, however, be
admitted by all. Some will urge that Confucianism
has been tried in China for some two thousand years
and has failed. " The answer to Confucianism " says
the cynic, " is China."[25]

Yet surely it would be futile to deny that Confucianism has been one of the principal factors that have
enabled China to live a continuous national life for a
longer period than any other nation existing to-day.
China during the past century has sunk low in the scale
of nations ; but is it fair to restrict ourselves to a consideration of those disastrous decades only, and to
ignore the glories of Han, T'ang and Sung ? Why is it
necessary to judge Confucianism by the criterion of the
harassed and humiliated China of to-day rather than
by that of the peaceful and glorious China that won
the enthusiastic admiration of observers in the less
civilised Europe of the seventeenth century ? Who is so
bold as to assert that never again can China rise to her

former height in the scale of civilised nations unless she discards Confucianism ?

If Confucianism is an evil thing, antagonistic to the healthy growth of a vigorous nationhood, why did it not destroy China long ago, before the modern nations of Europe came into existence ? If Confucianism is a deadly poison, how are we to account for the amazing fact that the poison has acted upon China like an elixir of life ?

Among those who shudderingly contemplate the melancholy state of contemporary Europe and perceive the colossal dangers threatening Western civilisation to-day, there are many who declare that " Christianity has failed." Such utterances are invariably met with the indignant reply "Christianity has not failed : it has never been tried." Yet the same people who are prompt to make this statement in defence of Christianity are the readiest to assert that " Confucianism has failed " and that the present state of China proves it. Are they prepared to demonstrate that Confucianism has been " tried " in China to a greater extent than Christianity has been " tried " in Europe ? No doubt it is true that if every Christian acted in strict and undeviating conformity with Christian principles, there would be perfect harmony and goodwill between Christian individuals and between Christian nations, and the Western world would to-day be under the sway of universal Love. But it is equally true to say that had every so-called Confucian conducted himself in accordance with Confucian principles, China would have established the supremacy of the rule of *Jên* ages ago,

and the ideal of *Wang Tao* would long since have become a sublime reality. If it be justifiable to say of
Christianity that it has not failed because it has never
been tried, it is no less justifiable to say the same of
Confucianism or—for that matter—of several of the
other great religious and ethical systems that have been
brought into existence for the guidance of erring human
nature and the elevation of the human spirit. It was
Nietzsche, I think, who remarked that there had been
only one Christian—and that He died on the Cross.
Has there been more than one Confucian? Perhaps
we may legitimately doubt whether there has been
even one. Between theory and practice there has always
been a great gulf fixed, both in the Christian West
and in the Confucian East.[26]

It was a modern sage of one of the youngest of great
States who declared not long ago that in spite of the
notorious evils of Chinese official life, China has perhaps " planted itself more consistently than any other
country on moral ideas, and this fact is not unrelated
to its long survival." Chinese civilisation, he went on
to say, has " numerous and grave peripheral faults "
but " it is likely to have a secret strength as long as the
Chinese refuse to ' drop their pilot ' "—as long as they
hold fast, " in spite of pressure from the West, to what
is best in the Confucian tradition."[27] These are wise
words and should be pondered by those Chinese who
would lightheartedly abandon their spiritual birthright.

Words of equal wisdom were spoken by one of my
distinguished predecessors in this lectureship a few
years ago. " A great nation," said Sir Henry Newbolt—

and he put these words in the forefront of his lecture—
" is one which is in possession of a territory, defined
but extensive, under long occupation and tillage,
capable of further development and increased production. . . . Such a nation is in the enjoyment of a spiritual
estate, an inherited culture, which is the result of its
common life, the sum of its characteristic attainments. . . . A loss of tradition, a degeneration of
culture, is an impoverishment which will lower its
strength and may in the end completely break it." He
adds that " Greece and Rome fell when their tradition
failed."[28]

The whole of the first paragraph of Sir Henry Newbolt's lecture may be earnestly commended to the attention of both Europeans and Chinese who are inclined
to underestimate the value and importance to China
of the *philosophia perennis* which we in the West call
Confucianism. His lecture had nothing to do with
China or Confucianism—its subject was English Poetry
—but this by no means lessens the significance of its
application to the cultural life of the Chinese people.

It is not only in recent times that people have arisen
in China who scorned and ridiculed the old traditions
and sought to destroy the old foundations of morality
and the old conception of life as an art. There is an
interesting and apposite passage in a book of the *Li
Chi* known as *Ching Chieh* (" Interpretations of the
Canon ") of which the following is a rough translation.

" The ceremonies which regulate the social relations check the rise of disorder and may be compared

with the dykes that check the overflow of the swollen river. Some think the old dykes useless and set to work to annihilate them : but they will suffer for this when the overflowing waters spread destruction far and wide. So it is with those who think the old rites and ceremonies useless. They seek to abolish them : but they will soon find themselves overwhelmed by the rising tide of wild confusion and disorder." [29]

Two thousand years, it may be, have passed since these words were written, and they have been verified during the past two decades of Chinese history.

Fortunately, as we have seen, the prospects of Confucianism in modern China are far from hopeless. Not only among scattered groups of Chinese colonists, not only in Manchuria, but in all parts of China, there are scholars, and great numbers who have no pretence to scholarship, who are tending the ancient fires. Dr. W. R. Inge, speaking of the strong influence of Neoplatonism on Christian philosophy, quotes a saying of a Neoplatonic disciple that the altars of Plotinus were still warm. We may say with equal truth that the altars of Confucius, too, are still warm, and I think we may add that it will be an evil day for China—and not for China only but for the whole world—when they grow stone cold.

NOTES

1. " I have been round the world," the bishop of London is reported to have said, " and I have seen at close quarters the other religions of the world. They have certainly got no candle to light them on their way." (Cf. Fausset, *A Modern Prelude*, p. 242.)

The bishop may have seen " the other religions " at close quarters, but that is not the same as seeing them *from within* ; and only from within could he have seen either the candles which he declares to be non-existent, or the sunlight that streams through their windows. By all means let us agree with those Christian writers who insist that Christianity cannot be estimated at its true value except by Christians ; but surely it is justifiable to remind them that it is they who are the outsiders when it is non-Christian creeds and systems that are under discussion. Bergson usefully reminds us of the extreme difficulty of achieving " *that intellectual sympathy* " which we call intuition. " The mind," he says, " has to do violence to itself, has to reverse the direction of the operation by which it habitually thinks, has perpetually to revise, or rather to recast, all its categories." Elsewhere in the same work he tells us that " from intuition one can pass to analysis, but not from analysis to intuition." (*An Introduction to Metaphysics*, London, 1913, pp. 59, 41.) Western critics of Oriental systems too often content themselves with analysis, but skill in analysis does not necessarily accompany the synthetic gift of intuition or intellectual sympathy.

CHAPTER II

1. For an account of the career and character of Chêng Hsiao-hsü (known in literary circles in China as Su-k'an) see my article in *The English Review*, June, 1932, pp. 643-51. His relations with the Manchu Court before and after the establishment of the new State of Manchuria are also described in my *Twilight in the Forbidden City* (Gollancz, 1934).

2. The following is the title of the book in Chinese characters in the handwriting of Chêng Hsiao-hsü himself :

3. *Hsiao Ching*, ix. See *Sacred Books of the East*, vol. iii, p. 476. Cf. *Shu Ching* (Legge's *Chinese Classics*, vol. iii, pt. ii, p. 283).

4. A well-known canonical statement of this doctrine occurs in *Mencius*, bk. ii, pt. i, ch. ii (see Legge, *op. cit.*, vol. ii, pp. 195–6). Cf. bk. vi, pt. i, ch. vii, 3 (Legge, *op. cit.*, p. 404), and bk. vi, pt. ii, ch. ii (Legge, *op. cit.*, p. 424).

5. See *The Philosophy of Plotinus*, 3rd ed., 1929, vol. ii, pp. 23–4, 178, and *God and the Astronomers* (London, 1933), pp. 274 and 298 f. It is " not surprising," says Dr. W. R. Inge, " that several saints are recorded to have wished that heaven and hell were blotted out, that they might serve God for Himself alone." He adds : " That virtue is its own reward, and that this reward is not deferred, is a belief which we have found vigorously asserted by great philosophers. . . . This is the noblest and truest way in which eternal life can be thought of. The more we can make it our own, the purer will our religion be fiom any selfish or mercenary taint." Modern Chinese who are neither theists nor Confucians, such as Dr. Hu Shih, are strong advocates of the view that virtue should be pursued for its own sake and not for fear of punishment or hope of reward. See Dr. Hu's article in *Hsin Ch'ing Nien* (*La Jeunesse*), vol. vi, No. 2, p. 97. Cf. A. Clutton-Brock, *The Ultimate Belief* (London, 1916), pp. 20 f., 26.

6. L. T. Hobhouse's warm tribute to this part of Confucian ethics is worth quoting. " The great Chinese classical writers in fact laid the foundation of a

distinct ethical and social ideal, in many ways analogous to the best teaching of the founders of spiritual religions, but different in its setting. . . . For example, man is not inherently bad and redeemed from evil only by divine grace. In himself he is potentially good, and the germs of goodness in him only need favourable circumstances, teaching, and effort to come to perfection. But they are developed, not to the greater glory of God, but to the maintenance of human life, that all along the rich valleys with their million homesteads the husbandman may reap the harvest he has sown in fields unstained by blood, that he may cherish wife and child and be nurtured by them in age, and pass duly honoured to the tomb ; that worthy officers be found to serve just and benevolent kings ; that wars may die away ; that crime may be repressed, not by punishment, but by the example of virtue ; in a word, that peaceful industry and happy family life undisturbed by civil jars, official corruption, royal avarice, and military ambition, may be the lot of one-third of the human race. Not the glory of God, but the peace of man is the aim ; not good fortune here nor salvation hereafter is the disciple's reward, but merely his best self independent of all that comes—righteousness for its own sake, benevolence because it is itself the best gift of heaven. Not the chaining up of human nature, but its full and harmonious development is the object of ethical training." *Morals in Evolution*, 2nd ed., 1908, pp. 176-7.

7. *Lun Yü* (" Analects of Confucius "), iv, 17.

8. *Ibid.*, iv, 24. Cf. L. Giles, *Sayings of Confucius* ("Wisdom of the East" series), p. 63. See also *Lun Yü*, v, 4.

9. *Ch'ang Shih Wên*, iv, 64 f. For another good modern Chinese analysis of the Confucian conception of the *chün-tzŭ*, readers of Chinese may consult the periodical *Ta Chung Hua*, vol. i, No. 9 : *K'ung Tzŭ Chiao I*, pp. 9 f.

10. Preaching at Westminster Abbey on October 18th, 1914, on the subject of the Great War then in progress, Dr. W. R. Inge spoke as follows : " If things go badly, we must remember that the true greatness of England has always been a moral and spiritual greatness founded above all perhaps on a definite and recognisable type of character—the lay religion of the English gentleman. This I most earnestly hope we shall always cherish, with its fine flowers of honourable dealing in war as well as in peace, of justice, kindliness and respect for the rights of others. It is the best thing that as a nation we have to give to the world." (*The Times*, October 19th, 1914.) See also H. W. Garrod (*The Religion of All Good Men*) quoted by M. L. Jacks in *The Hibbert Journal*, April, 1934, pp. 422 f.

This high praise of " the lay religion of the English gentleman," uttered (as Dr. Inge's remarks were) in a London pulpit, would perhaps have shocked the good man who declared that a " gentleman " was " the devil's imitation of a Christian." (See Temple's *Good Manners, An Address to the Semper Fidelis Society*, p. 8.)

11. See L. T. Hobhouse, *op. cit.*, ii, pp. 150, 160 f. Hobhouse had the greatest respect for Confucian

ethics, which he regarded as " one of the greatest and most influential doctrines of ethical conduct which the world has known."

12. The *Shuo Yüan* of Liu Hsiang (first century B.C.), xvi, p. 12(a).

13. *The Hibbert Journal*, October, 1923, pp. 8 f. In a leading article of December 11th, 1933, *The Times* observed that the League of Nations, during the thirteen years of its existence, had " rightly or wrongly gained a reputation for *spinning many words* which end, *not in action*, but in vague resolutions."

14. A leading article in *The North China Daily News* (Shanghai) of August 9th, 1915, drew a contrast between the Confucian *chün-tzŭ* or " gentleman " and the German conception of the " superman." The comparison was wholly in favour of the Chinese ideal, though allowance must be made for the fact that the article was written by an Englishman during the Great War. " In no other type of character," said the writer, referring to the Confucian *chün-tzŭ*, " do we find excelled those qualities of mildness, docility, peaceableness and politeness. And as a matter of fact the great majority of the Chinese race bear witness in their daily life to the effect of their high Confucian ideal. Their love of children, their dutifulness to parents, their care for the aged, their respect for learning, their scholarly instincts, the enduring sense of right and wrong which they possess, their loyalty to their word, their patience and temperance, their imperturbable coolness, and the many other good qualities they have

are very largely due to the teaching of the great Sage with regard to the ' superior man.' "

15. *Lun Yü*, v, 25.

16. It is said that at the meetings of the so-called " Oxford Groups " there is what has been described as " a rather wearisome reiteration of the slogan : ' I realised that if I wanted to change the world I must first change myself.' " (*Truth*, October 25th, 1933.) If this is one of the recognised teachings of the " Groups," they might do well to change their name from " Oxford " to " Confucian " Groups. It is strange that educated Englishmen should report, as though it were a new discovery, a truth which Confucius taught in China well over two thousand years ago.

17. See *Ta Hsüeh*, ch. vi, and *Chung Yung*, i, 3 (Legge, *Chinese Classics*, vol. i, pp. 366–7, 384 ; *Sacred Books of the East*, vol. xxviii, pp. 300, 408, 413).

18. Cf. Bacon : " Love of his country begins in a man's own house." (*De Aug. Sc.* quoted by A. F. Shand, *The Foundations of Character*, London : 1914, p. 91.) Regarding the emphasis laid on *discipline* in the Confucian system, it should be pointed out that the Confucian conception is better expressed by the Italian *disciplina*, which has been described by an English writer on Fascism as " self-respect combined with orderly unselfish behaviour as an outcome of an educated sense of one's responsibilities to society."

19. Burns's notion of what constitutes the " true pathos and sublime of human life " would of course be

anathema to our Communist philosophers of to-day, and therefore to many modern Chinese " intellectuals."

20. See *Shih Ching* ("Book of Poetry") II. i, iv (Legge, *Ch. Cl.* vol. iv, pt. ii, p. 252) ; *Chung Yung*, xv, 2 (Legge, *op. cit.*, vol. i, p. 396 ; *Sacred Books of the East*, vol. xxviii, p. 307).

21. *Lun Yü*, vi, 17.

22. J. Edkins, *Religion in China* (London : 1893), p. 120. Cf. *The Chinese Recorder*, vol. viii, 1877, p. 356, and *The Nineteenth Century and After*, 1913, p. 830.

23. *Op. cit.* (London : 1868), pp. 394, 591, etc.

24. Conrad Noel, *Byways of Belief* (London : 1912), p. 77. See also Younghusband's *Mutual Influence* (London : 1915), pp. 139, 143, and Edward Holmes's *What Is and What Might Be* (London : 1911), pp. 42 f., and the same writer's *Self-Realization* (London : 1927), p. 130 (note). Cf. *The Quest* quarterly, Jan. 1915, pp. 378–9.

25. *After Strange Gods* (London : 1934), p. 57. Cf. James Strachan, who tells us in Hastings' *Encyclopædia of Religion and Ethics* (vol. iv, p. 109) that "Jesus assumes in many indirect ways the natural sinfulness of the human heart."

26. *Realm of Ends* (Cambridge : 1911), p. 369.

27. *Mind*, July, 1912, p. 433. Sir Henry Jones would also have sided with Confucius and Mencius on the question of the inherent goodness of human nature. See his admirable discussion of the nature of moral evil in his *A Faith that Enquires*, pp. 244–55. Dr. H. A.

Oc

Giles in his *Confucianism and its Rivals* (London : 1915), pp. 83–95 f., points out that the germ of the Confucian view is to be found in pre-Confucian literature.

28. Mencius's teaching on this subject is dealt with by Dr. J. Legge in his *Chinese Classics*, vol. ii (2nd ed.), pp. 57 f. He admits that " to many Christian readers " Mencius's belief in the goodness of human nature " proves a stumbling-block and offence " ; but he himself, though a Christian missionary, agrees with Mencius and summons Bishop Butler as a strong witness on the same side. Cf. *The Hibbert Journal*, October, 1923, pp. 44 f., and Massingham's *Heritage of Man*, pp. 141 f.

29. According to a contemporary student of early Chinese philosophy, Mr. Liu Nien-ch'in, the famous chapter in which the theory of the radical badness of man's nature is pressed with much argumentative force was not written by Hsün-K'uang but was added by a later hand, probably during the first century B.C. In his opinion, the chapter does not represent Hsün K'uang's views, and is clearly a forgery. Professor E. H. Parker had already remarked that the chapter is " entirely different in style and vigour " from the other chapters of Hsün K'uang's book and attributed this to its having been written " under stress of violent emotion." I have dealt with this subject in my article on " Ancient Chinese Philosophy " in *The Chinese Social and Political Science Review*, April, 1923.

30. Speaking at a conference of the National Council for Mental Hygiene, as recently as November 22nd,

1933, the Regius Professor of Physic at Cambridge (Dr. W. Langdon Brown) observed that " disorders of the pituitary glands may make for boastfulness, lying, thieving and an insatiable craving for the limelight. Too little thyroid gland may render a man melancholy and suspicious, too much may make a woman excitable, intransigent, even insane." Human nature, say the Confucians, is fundamentally good but may be deflected from goodness by a bad education or environment. But what if the "badness" be due to the erratic working of a pituitary or thyroid gland? The subject is a perplexing one for the moral philosophers of all creeds and systems, not only for Confucian thinkers.

31. *Mencius*, bk. iv, pt. ii, ch. xii. (Legge, *op. cit.*, p. 322). For a reference to the "child-heart" of the Manchu emperor Kao Tsung (Ch'ien-Lung), see my *Twilight in the Forbidden City*, p. 173.

32. Legge, *The Chinese Classics*, vol. ii (2nd ed., 1895), p. 70. William McDougall in his *Character and The Conduct of Life* (London : 1927, p. 175) observes that the self-respect of the modern child " is no longer undermined from the outset by the pernicious doctrine that he is by nature a little blackguard. Rather, he is brought up on the assumption that he is by nature good, that in any decently organised society he will naturally seek the good, the true and the beautiful. That is a great gain." The assumption referred to would meet with the whole-hearted acceptance of the Confucian School, and is indeed expressly taught by it, even to the emphasis laid on " decently organised society."

Cf. Wingfield-Stratford's *The Reconstruction of Mind* (London, 4th impr., 1922), pp. xviii, 50, 51.

33. *Our Friend John Burroughs*, by Clara Barrus (Boston : 1914), p. 8.

34. F. C. Prescott, *The Poetic Mind* (New York : 1922), p. 58. A writer in *The Modern Churchman* (July, 1922, p. 222) asks how the transition can be made from the religion of the child to the religion of the adult. " We suppose," he says, " the only means are that the adult should retain certain characteristics of the child—sincerity, sympathy, curiosity, eagerness, imagination, seriousness, lightness of touch, and so on. Can it be done ? "

35. Quoted in *The Times*, November 20th, 1933.

36. *Lun Yü*, vii, 24.

37. *Lun Yü*, i, vi, vii, *Li Chi*, bk. xvii (" Record of Music "), section iii, 5.

38. *The Times*, November 10th, 1933.

39. *Shuo Yüan*, ch. xx, p. 13 (b).

40. *Lun Yü*, ix, 28.

41. *Lun Yü*, xiii, 19.

42. *Jên* and *I* are often brought into collocation, when *Jên* is said to be the love of one's fellow-men and *I* is self-discipline. *Jên* is also described as the inner principle which manifests itself outwardly in *I*. H. A. Giles (*Dictionary*, 5627) defines *Jên* as " an inward and spiritual love for all mankind, of which *I* is the outward and visible manifestation, best rendered by ' charity ' in its theological sense. Goodness, humanity, kindness, mercy."

43. *Lun Yü*, xii. 5.

44. The Right Rev. Lord William Gascoyne-Cecil (bishop of Exeter) in *Changing China* (London : 1910), p. 220. The history of the European races, up to and including the last few months, suggests doubts as to whether the doctrine in question, which Lord William has declared to be "solely Christian," has yet won general acceptance, even in Christendom. Negroes in America, Japanese and Chinese in the Far East, and Jews in Germany, are said to be among those who harbour such doubts.

45. *The Origin and Growth of the Moral Instinct* (London : 1898), vol. i, pp. 402–3.

46. *Mencius*, bk. ii, pt. i, ch. ii.

47. *Lun Yü*, xv, 23.

48. Legge, *op. cit.*, vol. i, p. 301.

49. *Sayings of Confucius* ("Wisdom of the East" series), p. 69.

50. Cf. *Lun Yü*, v, 11 ; *Chung Yung*, xiii, 3–4 ; xiv ; *Ta Hsüeh*, ch. x.

51. *Gems of Chinese Literature* (Shanghai : 1922), p. 6, and *Confucianism and its Rivals* (London : 1915), p. 85. A valuable recent anthology of the various enunciations of the principle in different times and places may be found in *A Book of the Golden Rule*, by Jane T. Stoddart (London : 1933).

52. *A Short History of Morals* (London : 1920), pp. 154–5.

53. One example occurs in *Mencius*, book vii, pt. i,

ch. xvii, and another in the *Chung Yung*, ch. xx, 17. The *negative* form of the Golden Rule is often found in early Christian literature. See Hastings, *Encycl. of Religion and Ethics*, vol. vi, pp. 310 f.

54. Legge, *op. cit.*, vol. i, p. 49.

55. G. K. Chesterton, *St. Thomas Aquinas* (London : 1933), p. 209.

56. Benjamin Apthorp Gould, in *War Thoughts of an Optimist*. Cf. Irving Babbitt : " We have not as yet set up, like revolutionary France, as the Christ of Nations, but during the late war we liked to look on ourselves as at least the Sir Galahad of Nations." (*Democracy and Leadership* : Boston and New York : 1924, p. 269.)

57. That some missionaries have believed that the Golden Rule was peculiar to Christianity is shown in an amusing story told by Dr. J. B. Pratt in his *India and its Faiths* (London : 1916, p. 430). When confronted by Shivanath Shastri, the leader of the Brahmo Samaj, with the Golden Rule in Confucius and in the Talmud, a group of missionaries expressed surprise, but finally got out of the difficulty by saying, " Ah well, you know the Devil, too, can inspire men to write the truth." To which Mr. Shastri answered, " Gentlemen, you have disarmed me ; there is nothing I can reply to that ! "

58. Cf. D. T. Suzuki, *Chinese Philosophy*, pp. 94, 99.

59. It should be explained that the " heresies " of Mo Tzŭ are not by any means regarded with equanimity by all modern scholars in China. An able and thoughtful writer of our own time, Mr. Liu I-chêng,

has expressed the view that the strictures of Mencius were not undeserved, and that Mo Ti's doctrine of " universal love " was, in fact, dangerous to society and destructive of the special love due to kith and kin. In his opinion it is no accidental circumstance that the period of growing enthusiasm for Mo Ti has precisely synchronised with the decay of filial piety and the increasing tendency to cast off the old social and family bonds. (See *The Chinese Social and Political Science Review*, April, 1923, in which I have dealt with this subject.) Mr. Liu would find a supporter in the person of Mr. G. K. Chesterton, who very properly rejects the notion that we can love all men equally. " To speak of having the same kind of regard " for two different people " is about as sensible as asking a man whether he prefers chrysanthemums or billiards. Christ did not love humanity ; He never said He loved humanity ; He loved men. Neither He nor anyone else can love humanity ; it is like loving a gigantic centipede." (*Tolstoy and the Cult of Simplicity* in " Twelve Types," London : 1910, p. 164.) Mo Ti's critics might consider themselves justified in declaring that he loved a gigantic centipede.

60. *Lun Yü*, ix, 25.

61. *Lun Yü*, xv, 8. The " man of true virtue " is he who possesses *jên*—the quality mentioned in the eighth text.

62. *The Name and Nature of Poetry* (Cambridge : 1933), p. 36.

63. *Lun Yü*, iv, 10.

64. *Lun Yü*, iv, 8.

65. *Lun Yü*, xv, 38.

66. *North China Standard*, Peking, Jan. 25th, 1923.

67. *The Discourses and Sayings of Confucius* (Shanghai : 1898), p. 141.

68. For some account of the character and personality of Ku Hung-ming, see my *Twilight in the Forbidden City*, pp. 88–9, 92, 345–7, 465 (note 16).

69. Legge, *op. cit.*, vol. i, p. 305.

70. Lyall, *The Sayings of Confucius* (London : 1909), p. 87.

71. The following words are those of Professor Hsü Shih-lien, whose English book entitled *The Political Philosophy of Confucianism* (London : 1932) is well worthy of study.

" There was no aristocracy in education. The *Li Chi* declares that ' even the eldest son of the emperor by his legitimate queen is only an ordinary student.' According to the ' Royal Regulation,' the sons of the emperor, the princes, and the officials should study at the same university with the students chosen from among the common people ; and they should be divided into classes not by ranks but by ages. This system is extremely sane and democratic. . . . In Chinese society, until recently, scholars were generally regarded by the people of their locality as their representatives in public affairs. This was a practical illustration of the influence of Confucian teachings." (*Op. cit.*, p. 195.)

CHAPTER III

1. The following words are those of a contemporary Chinese sociologist, Mr. Yung-Chi Hoe (*China Critic,* vol. iii, No. 43) : " Filial piety is the alpha and omega of his [Confucius's] ethics. It includes and logically presupposes every other virtue under heaven. Thus, honesty, justice, courage, self-control, modesty and loyalty all come under the single rubric of devotion to parents."

The following observations on our term " filial piety " are by Mr. M. M. Dawson (*The Ethics of Confucius,* New York and London : 1915, p. 156) : " It is remarkable and significant that it should in these modern days be necessary to say ' filial piety.' ' Pietas ' originally signified reverent devotion to parents and unflagging service of them. Through this, the meaning ' service of the Heavenly Father ' has been derived. Meanwhile the original meaning of the word has been lost—indeed, as a serious duty, the very thing itself is near to have been lost—and it is now requisite to use the tautology ' filial piety ' to express the idea for which ' piety ' alone once stood."

2. " The piety of the ancient Chinese . . . did not solely or even primarily consist in sacrifices to the spirits of the dead. It called for the greatest reverence and devotion while the parent is yet living. Its most important phase, indeed, was the obligation it imposed to live an honourable and creditable life, that the parents might not have occasion to blush for their offspring."

M. M. Dawson, *op. cit.*, p. 157. Cf. Dr. Hu Shih, *The Chinese Renaissance* (Chicago : 1934), p. 82.

3. *Lun Yü*, ii. 6.

4. " Nimis e natura dictum est nescio quem filios invenisse tortorem . . . in quo Euripidis mei sententiam probo, qui carentem liberis infortunio dixit esse felicem." Boethius, *Consol. Phil.*, III, vii. The passage in Euripides to which he referred is in the *Andromache*, 418–20 :

πᾶσι δ᾽ἀνθρώποις ἄρ᾽ ἦν
ψυχὴ τέκν᾽ ὅστις δ᾽αὖτ᾽ ἄπειρος ὢν ψέγει,
ἧσσον μὲν ἀλγεῖ, δυστυχῶν δ᾽εὐδαιμονεῖ.

5. See *Ta Hsüeh*, ch. ix. (Legge, *op. cit.*, vol. i, p. 370).

6. *Mencius*, bk. vi, pt. ii, ch. ii, 4.

7. See *Twilight in the Forbidden City*, pp. 25–33.

8. The following apposite passage occurs in an article by Felix Adler on " Incompatibility in the Personal Relations " in *The Standard* (New York) vol. xi, No. 9, May, 1925, p. 262. " I know of a young radical who puts his thoughts in this wise : Why should I be grateful to my parents ? Gratitude is supposed to be due to a benefactor. A benefactor is one who intends to benefit another. But my parents had no intention of benefiting me. They had no idea of what kind of being I might turn out to be." In this " young radical "— presumably an American—Dr. Hu Shih would meet a kindred spirit. For a further discussion of the subject by this able and distinguished leader of modern thought in China, see *The Chinese Renaissance* (Chicago : 1934), pp. 102 f.

9. It would be easy to give examples from the European and American press of incidents which would fully justify Confucian China, from the standpoint of its own ethical standards, in denouncing Western civilisation. I will give three illustrations taken from recent newspapers.

An army reservist, aged twenty-five, was charged at Highgate with causing grievous bodily harm to his father. " For the last three weeks he had been drinking heavily. On Saturday his father remonstrated with him, and he then threatened to ' bash ' him. On Sunday evening, without any provocation, he struck his father, rendering him unconscious, and causing concussion of the brain."

The prisoner when questioned by the magistrate (Sir Alfred Reynolds) explained that his father had insulted him.

" Has a father no right to rebuke his son ? " asked the magistrate.

" Of course not," replied the prisoner.

Magistrate : " It is the spirit of the age. You will be sentenced to six weeks' hard labour."

In China there was a time, not long ago, when a son who struck his father would have been deemed to have deserved the death-penalty. Although even in China there is to-day a change coming over " the spirit of the age," Chinese public opinion would be greatly shocked if the penalty imposed for such a crime were no more than six weeks' hard labour.

The second case, reported from Germany, was

referred to in the *Evening Standard* (London) of June 28th, 1933.

" Dr. Heinrich Held, son of the former Bavarian premier, was arrested yesterday because he would not betray his father to the Nazi authorities. He is reported to have been interned in the notorious concentration camp originally intended only for Communists at Dachau, near Munich. Herr Held senior is believed to be in a nursing home. Dr. Heinrich Held is an engineer by profession and has never played any part in politics."

The third case is reported from Soviet Russia, in a Russian telegram dated May 21st, 1934.

" Pronya Kolibin is the latest Communist ' hero.' At the age of thirteen he has won the praise of the Soviet authorities for reporting to them that his mother was stealing grain from a collective farm in a district near Moscow. Theft of this grain is a crime punishable by death.

" The Soviet authorities have given Pronya a cash reward for betraying his mother. The boy recorded his mother's misdeeds in verse which is published in the newspaper *Pravda*.

" It is not stated whether the mother was using the stolen grain to help feed her children."

(*Morning Post*, May 22nd, 1934.)

Confucian China would not expect a son to betray his father or his mother, and would despise him if he did. But " Mo-têng " China is beginning to be ashamed of its "barbaric" past, and may soon fall into line with the civilised West.

10. See Legge, *op. cit.*, vol. ii, pp. 72–3.

CHAPTER IV

1. Yung-Chi Hoe, *From Family to State* ("The China Critic," vol. iii, No. 43).

2. See *Twilight in the Forbidden City*, p. 180.

3. *The Lore of Cathay* (New York : 1901), p. 287.

4. See *Twilight in the Forbidden City*, ch. xii, p. 181, and note 3, p. 468.

5. "Manifesto : Being the Book of the Federation of Progressive Societies and Individuals" (London : 1934), pp. 146–7.

6. *Ibid.*, p. 143.

7. One of the wisest and best-equipped students of modern China, Father Léon Wieger, wrote in 1921 as follows : "La foi aveugle aux paroles du maître n'est pas encore étiente, et ne s'éteindra pas de si tôt, dans le pays de Confucius " (*Chine Moderne* : tome i : *Moralisme*, Preface). In a chapter on "Education in China" which I contributed to *The Year Book of Education*, 1932, edited by Lord Eustace Percy, I wrote as follows : "The bewildered onlooker—especially if he be a foreigner—is likely to jump to the conclusion that the wild doings of schoolboys and students and the scant respect paid to schoolmasters and college professors and presidents indicate that the traditional Chinese respect

for learning and the old ethical relationship between master and pupil are things of the past. Yet this would be a hasty judgment. . . . In spite of all this it is undoubtedly true, though it may appear paradoxical to say so, that in China to-day there is a greater zeal for learning, a keener intellectual curiosity and a more genuine thirst for knowledge than have been known in the country for hundreds of years."

CHAPTER V

1. *History of Chinese Political Thought* (London : 1930), pp. 153–5. I have italicised sentences to which special attention is drawn.

2. *Roman Ideas of Deity* (London : 1914), p. 27. See also Maine's *Ancient Law* (London : The New Universal Library), pp. 158–9, 160.

3. Cf. Maine, *op. cit.*, pp. 104, 153 f., 158 f. See also p. 214, where Maine says : " The life of each citizen is not regarded [in Ancient Law] as limited by birth and death ; it is but a continuation of the existence of his forefathers, and it will be prolonged in the existence of his descendants." See also my *Lion and Dragon in Northern China* (London : 1910), pp. 258 f., 276 f., 318 f., and an interesting article on " The Meaning of Chinese Ancestor Worship " by J. T. Addison in *The Chinese Recorder* (Shanghai), vol. lv, No. 9, Sept., 1924, pp. 592 f.

4. The Rev. Conrad Noel, in *Byways of Belief* (London :

1912), pp. 292–3. Cf. *God and the War*, by Archdeacon Paterson-Smyth, pp. 127 f. ; and Bishop Henson's *Sermons in War-Time*, p. 126. In a letter to *The Times* of Jan. 4th, 1915, the latter confessed to " a measure of apprehension at the rapid development of devotion connected with the departed " among members of the Church of England. It is unnecessary to refer to similar beliefs and practices in the Church of Rome ; but a Chinese " ancestor-worshipper " might be excused for asking why a cardinal of that Church may pray to the spirit of his dead mother without being accused of idolatry or of elevating his parent to godship, whereas a Chinese peasant is reproved if he pays similar reverence to the spirits of his own loved and honoured dead. (For the case referred to, see *The Nineteenth Century and After*, August, 1910, p. 273.)

5. With regard to the attitude of Christian missionaries in China towards the " idolatry " of the ancestral tablet, a touching and significant story is told by the Right Rev. Lord William Gascoyne-Cecil in his *Changing China* (London : 1910), pp. 159–60.

6. It is not surprising that local and domestic loyalties have had a tenacious existence in China and are only very gradually giving way to more comprehensive loyalties. " It is only a law of nature," as Mr. T. S. Eliot has recently said, " that local patriotism, when it represents a distinct tradition and culture, takes precedence over a more abstract national patriotism." (*After Strange Gods*, London : 1934, p. 20.) Cf. McDougall's *The Group Mind* (Cambridge : 1920), p. 150.

See also Lionel Curtis, *Civitas Dei* (London : 1934), p. 275. Cf. the very important observations of Dr. Hu Shih in his recent book *The Chinese Renaissance*, already cited, pp. 102–10.

7. *The Hibbert Journal*, Jan. 1923, p. 308. Bertrand Russell's remarks are also noteworthy. " The harm that is done at present by biological groupings is undeniable, but I do not think the social problem can be solved by ignoring the instincts which produce those groupings. . . . Nationalism also perhaps has its place, though clearly armies and navies are an undesirable expression of it, and its proper sphere is cultural rather than political. Human beings can be greatly changed by institutions and education, but if they are changed in such a way as to thwart fundamental instincts, the result is a loss of vigour." (*Sceptical Essays*, London : 1928, pp. 230–1.)

8. " The two institutions," says Sir Charles Petrie, " which had for centuries held Chinese society together were the throne and the family, and the disappearance of the former was soon followed by the disappearance of the latter. The missionaries, needless to say, with a few notable exceptions, accelerated the good work of breaking with tradition, and so receptive did they find the minds of their pupils that within fifteen years of the advent of the republic they were streaming to the coast with their mission-stations in flames behind them." (*Monarchy*, London : 1933, p. 252.) The reference is to the anti-foreign outbursts of 1925–29. For the part taken by Christian missionaries in preparing the way for revolution, see chapter x.

CHAPTER VI

1. I dealt with the subject of the conditional nature of the power vested in the Chinese emperors in an article entitled " Political Sovereignty in China " published in *The Nineteenth Century and After*, July, 1912. For Lord Morley's criticism of Hume's views on the doctrine of non-resistance, see *On Compromise* (London : 1923 ed.), pp. 118 f.

2. *Mencius*, bk. i, pt. ii, ch. vi.

3. *Ibid.*, bk. i, pt. ii, ch. viii.

4. *Ibid.*, bk. vii, pt. ii, ch. xiv. These democratic teachings of Mencius were among those which, in defiance of the opinion of the first emperor of the Ming dynasty, I endeavoured to impress upon the mind of the last emperor of the dynasty that succeeded it. See *Twilight in the Forbidden City*, pp. 233, 246–8.

5. *Ta Hsüeh*, x, 3, 5.

6. *Shu Ching*, pt. v, bk. i, ii. The words are quoted from the *Shu Ching* in *Mencius*, bk. v, pt. i, ch. v.

7. These words are quoted by the Rev. R. D. Richardson in *The Modern Churchman*, vol. xxiii, Nos. 5, 6 and 7, October, 1933, p. 437.

8. Liu Hsiang, *Shuo Yüan*, ch. viii, p. 1.

9. *Ibid.*, ch. ix, p. 2.

10. Duke Ching of Ch'i reigned from about 547 to 490 B.C. See references to his doings in *Mencius* (Legge, *op. cit.*, vol. ii, p. 158 f. and elsewhere). He is there shown to have listened to the good advice of his minister Yen Ying, who died 493 B.C. (See H. A.

Pc

Giles, *Biograph. Dict.*, No. 2483.) Incidentally, this story gives indirect evidence of what we know from other sources, that human sacrifices were not unknown in the China of the age immediately preceding that of Confucius.

11. Liu Hsiang, *Hsin Hsü*, ch. ii, pp. 7–8.

12. *Shuo Yüan*, ch. xii, p. 11 (*b*). Tortoises were used in ancient China for purposes of divination, and human blood was sometimes mingled with the molten metal of important bells. Drums and bells were used to convey signals to the troops in battle.

13. *Hsin Hsü*, ch. ii, pp. 4 (*b*), 5.

14. *Shuo Yüan*, ch. i, p. 5 (*b*).

15. *Mencius*, bk. i, pt. ii, ch. x.

16. See *Modern China* by S. G. Cheng (London : 1919), p. 124.

CHAPTER VII

1. That this is the true Confucian teaching is acknowledged by Dr. Legge. See his *Chinese Classics*, vol. i, pp. 51–3, 414 f. A commentator on the *I Ching* (" Book of Changes ") described the Sage as *jên lei chih shou*—the head or leader among mankind.

2. Le Comte's *Memoirs and Remarks*, Engl. ed., London : 1738, p. 201.

3. For an account of the Chinese cult of military heroes, pre-eminent among whom are Kuan Ti and Yo Fei, see my articles in *The New China Review* (Shanghai), vol. iii, Nos. 1 and 2.

4. An account of the posthumous honours conferred on Confucius, and of the Confucian cult in general, may be found in *The Origin and Development of the State Cult of Confucius*, by John K. Shryock (New York : 1932).

5. *Confucianism and its Rivals* (Hibbert Lecture, 1914), p. 258. A similar misunderstanding is revealed in the *Reports of the World Missionary Conference, 1910*, Vol. i, pp. 15 f.

6. *Changing China* (London : 1910), pp. 300–1. The " eminent missionary " who thought that by making Confucius " equal to Heaven and Earth " the Government had made a god of him, seems to have been less familiar with the Chinese classics than he should have been. A knowledge of the *Chung Yung* and a comprehension of its mystical ideas concerning the ideal Sage who was identified with Confucius, would have saved him from this error. See chapter xxxi of that classic (translated by Legge, *Chinese Classics*, vol. i, p. 429). The most recent of the Western writers on Confucianism who have fallen into the error of supposing that Confucius, early in this century, was elevated to godhead by imperial decree, is Dr. B. S. Bonsall. (See his book *Confucianism and Taoism*, London : 1934, p. 67.) He is also in error in describing the reverence paid to Confucius and the leading exponents of his system as " worship." The nearest Western analogy to the cult of Confucius is the cult of the Saints in Christendom. Catholics will not admit that St. Thomas Aquinas is " worshipped " as a god, or that the Virgin is "worshipped" as a goddess :

hence their objection to the use of the word " worship " in this connection, which they prefer to replace by " adoration." Confucians have just as much right to object to the cult of their Sage being described as " worship." Dr. Bonsall also makes the surprising statement (p. 68) that the alleged elevation of Confucius to godhead was " a reply to the Western deification of Jesus." There is no reason whatever to suppose that the scholars who were entrusted with the drafting of the edict in question (which simply recognised Confucius as the ideal Sage of the *Chung Yung*) were influenced in any way by their knowledge of the Christian doctrine of the Godhead of Christ.

7. *Sacred Books of the East*, vol. xxviii, p. 88. See also above, pp. 48–9.

8. It is true that the scholarly viceroy Chang Chih-tung (born 1835) declared that Confucianism was a religion, but this was because he had occasion to compare it with, and defend it against, other systems which were definitely religious, such as Christianity and Buddhism. In his eyes, Confucianism was " a holy religion which is absolutely unvarying and a perfect standard of conduct . . . embodying the pure law of God above with the fullest recognition of human relationships " (H. A. Giles, *Gems of Chinese Literature*, p. 266). On this subject, see also Dr. Hu Shih, *The Chinese Renaissance*, pp. 88 f.

9. Chang Chih-tung seems to have preferred *shêng chiao*—" holy teaching."

10. " Confucius," as most people know, is a latinisa-
tion of K'ung Fu Tzŭ—" the Master K'ung." K'ung
was the Sage's surname.

11. These facts are recognised in missionary circles.
The following note appears in *China's Millions* (the
organ of the China Inland Mission), September, 1917,
p. 108. " It is a noteworthy fact that it is only since the
advent of Christianity into China that what we call
Confucianism has begun to be designated by the name
of *K'ung Chiao* instead of the more ancient and imper-
sonal term *Ju Chiao*, which may be translated as the
Literary Cult."
The fact that the Confucian classics are included by
Western scholars in their collections of " The Sacred
Books of the East " has often given rise to the question,
" To what extent, if at all, is the Confucian canon
entitled to be called Religious or Sacred ? " The question has been well answered by the Rev. Gilbert
Walshe in the periodical *China*.
" It may be asked why these should be adduced
under the head of ' *Religious* literature,' when, as a
matter of fact, they are really politico-moral, and the
answer is that from these works alone, are we able to
glean the history of Religion in China, and that they,
especially the historical works, are instinct with religious feeling. The argument which underlies the whole
Confucian library is the triumph of virtue, and its
antithesis—the nemesis which overtakes vice, as illustrated by the lives of kings and lesser rulers ; and to a
corresponding degree, in the case of the people

generally. A very few quotations will be sufficient to show that not mere morality is here referred to, but that the sanctions of Religion are urged as a motive to Righteousness—the will of Heaven is the final Court of Appeal " (*China*, July, 1914, p. 751).

12. See *Mencius*, iii, i, v, 3. (Legge, *op. cit.*, vol. ii, p. 258) and vii, ii, xxvi, 1 (*ibid.*, p. 491). It is only in the second of these passages that Mencius himself is represented as speaking of the orthodox doctrine as *ju*.

13. The history and various meanings of *ju* have been ably investigated by modern Japanese students and also by a Chinese scholar of our own time named Chang Shou-lin. The latter, who acknowledges his indebtedness to his Japanese predecessors in this line of research, published four interesting articles on the subject in the Peking Chinese newspaper *Ch'ên Pao* of March 12–15, 1928. He thinks that the term *ju* when first applied to the orthodox scholars as a term of ridicule or abuse may have had some reference to the dress and manners of the latter ; and he suggests that they may have worn a distinctive uniform—a sort of academic costume.

14. See Dr. W. R. Inge, *God and the Astronomers* (London : 1933), p. 257.

15. Quoted by Alfred Noyes, *The Unknown God* (London : 1934), p. 123.

16. Legge, *op. cit.*, vol. iii, pt. ii, p. 332.

17. *Op. cit.*, vol. ii, p. 155. It may be that if Confucius had been able to use modern phraseology he might, when speaking philosophically, have adopted some

such term as " totality of values " rather than a term so liable to misuse and misunderstanding as " T'ien " or " God." The Confucian view is perhaps more easily reconcilable with that of such modern scholars as Dr. Kirsopp Lake than with that of traditional Christianity. (See that able and courageous writer's *The Religion of Yesterday and To-morrow*, and cf. his *Paul, His Heritage and Legacy* [London : 1934], pp. 85 f.)

18. Dr. C. A. Alington, as reported in the *Daily Telegraph*, June 10, 1933.

19. See above, pp. 69–70.

20. There is some reason to suspect that human sacrifices to secure good crops were once as common in China as they were up to a recent date in West Africa, Bengal and elsewhere. The observations made on this subject by Mr. E. O. James in his *Origins of Sacrifice* (London : 1933), pp. 96 f., 284 f. might be applied with little change of language to primitive conditions in China. Cf. also René Grousset's *China* (Engl. transl., London : 1934), pp. 16, 31 f.

21. My interpretation of the passage (*Lun Yü*, bk. iii, ch. xiii) is not that of the Chinese commentators, some of whom have a far-fetched explanation of the question put by Wang-sun Chia. Legge (*Chinese Classics*, vol. i, p. 159), translates the whole passage thus :

" Wang-sun Chia asked, saying ' What is the meaning of the saying " It is better to pay court to the furnace than to the south-west corner " ? '

"The Master said, 'Not so. He who offends against Heaven has none to whom he can pray.'"

The phrase " not so," though it seems to be a literal translation of the Chinese *pu jan*, is hardly an intelligible reply to the question. Legge (and many of his Chinese predecessors) seem to have missed the point of both question and answer.

22. See also the most recent utterances by Dr. Hu Shih on this subject in his work *The Chinese Renaissance*, pp. 81 f.

23. *Lun Yü*, bk. vi, ch. xx. It may be said, perhaps rightly, that the term " agnostic humanist " is self-contradictory. The humanist as such, as Mr. T. S. Eliot has pointed out, " is not concerned with philosophical foundations." (See *Selected Essays*, London : 1932, pp. 436 f.). Confucius was a humanist but something more. He would have admitted, I think, that " humanism is not enough." Dr. C. C. J. Webb, in his *Religion and Theism* (London : 1934) says that Confucianism (and certain other supposedly non-theistic systems) are really theistic without knowing it. That Confucianism is " really theistic " I believe to be true ; that it is " theistic without knowing it " is open to question.

24. Legge *op. cit.*, vol. i, p. 191. Moreover, as Mr. Herlee Glessner Creel points out in his article " Was Confucius Agnostic ? " in *T'oung Pao*, vol. xxix, Nos. 1–3, 1932, p. 85, the important character *yüan* does not, in this and other passages, mean " to keep aloof from "

but denotes " the sort of austere respect which should exist between parents and children." I am glad to take this opportunity of expressing my general agreement with Mr. Creel in the conclusions arrived at by him in his valuable article. He gives excellent reasons for dissenting from the common assumption that Confucius limited " his view and his interests purely to the human realm, paying not the slightest heed to things ' metaphysical.' " He closes his study with the following words : " It is impossible to understand Confucius unless we recognise that for him, as surely as for the priests and prophets of Israel, ethics, politics and the whole of life were inseparable from their cosmic and religious background."

25. For Dr. Legge's comments on this passage, see his *Chinese Classics*, vol. i, p. 99. Modern critics hold that the *Chia Yü* as we have it dates from about 700 years after the time of Confucius—say the third century of our era. It is impossible to say whether any part of its contents was handed down from the Confucian age. The words ascribed to Confucius in this passage may be compared with the more emphatic pronouncement of Socrates as recorded by Eusebius—" the secrets of nature are above us, and the conditions after death nothing to us, but the affairs of human life alone concern us." (Blakeney's *Apology of Socrates*, London : 1929, pp. 181–2. The translation is Gifford's. Cf. also p. 19.)

26. Liu Hsiang, *Hsin Hsü*, ch. i, p. 7.

27. *Ibid.*, ch. iv, p. 4.

28. *Li Chi*, book xxii. (See *Sacred Books of the East*, vol. xxviii, pp. 236–7.)

29. Le Comte's *Memoirs and Remarks*, London, 1738, pp. 199–200.

30. See my article on " The Religious Future of China " in *The Nineteenth Century and After*, November, 1913, p. 920.

31. Dr. Legge declares that the lack of religion in Confucian thought " has left the people in the main to become an easy prey to the idolatrous fooleries of Buddhism." I disagree with Dr. Legge in his contemptuous estimate of Buddhism (which, as far as I know, he made no serious attempt to understand), but it is undoubtedly true that for great numbers of the Chinese people the religious side of Confucianism has proved inadequate or too austere for their needs, and they have turned to Buddhism. They have usually done so without abandoning Confucianism as a rule of life.

32. It should be noted that the early Jesuit missionaries did not content themselves with praising the ethics of Confucius. They also denied that his philosophy was atheistic. Dr. Virgile Pinot has recently reminded us that the Jesuits held " que les philosophies chinois ne sont pas athées, et que la philosophie et l'athéisme ne peuvent se concilier ni en Chine ni en France,"—and that Voltaire somewhat reluctantly concurred in their judgment on this matter. (*La Chine et La Formation de l'Esprit Philosophique en France 1640–1740*, Paris : 1932.)

33. A Chinese writer in a periodical called the *Ta*

Chung Hua (vol. i, No. 9, 1915, p. 3), discussed the question of Confucianism and Religion in an interesting manner. He observed that it was usual to test whether a system were a religion or not by enquiring (1) whether it had a doctrine of the spiritual world, and (2) whether it possessed religious rites and ceremonies. But the proper test, he says, is whether or not it has a " world-saving method " (*chiu shih chih fang-fa*). If this test be applied to Confucianism, he concludes, it is discovered to be a religion.

But of course the phrase " world-saving method " is in itself ambiguous, both in English and in Chinese. It may refer to " this world," in which case Socialism, Fascism, Communism, and many other " isms " may all claim to be religions, or its emphasis may be on the next world. If it be argued that a " method " which " saves " humanity in this world will also " save " it in the next, we may remind ourselves that the world, like an individual, may conceivably " save itself " and " lose its own soul."

Julian Huxley has recently observed that " we are witnessing the dawn of a struggle, not between science and religion, but between the God-religions and social-religions."

34. Cicero declared that " Socrates was the first to fetch down philosophy from heaven and bring it into the cities and houses of men, compelling them to enquire about life, and morality, and good and evil." (See Blakeney, *op. cit.*, p. 182.) But Cicero had never heard of Confucius, who died about nine years before

Socrates was born. (Confucius died 479 B.C., Socrates was born about 470.)

35. *Religion in China* (London : 1893), p. 75. I have italicised one sentence. The passage is discussed in my *Chinese Appeal to Christendom Concerning Christian Missions* (written under the pen-name of Lin Shao-yang), London, 1911, pp. 286–7. Mr. J. M. Robertson's opinion of Chinese ethics, both in theory and in practice, was very high. " If general clearness of vision," he says, " as to what is ' good ' in private and public conduct be any criterion of an ethical basis, the moralists of ancient China must be rated at least as high as any in antiquity, theistic or otherwise. It would be no ill discipline to add the study of their ethics to that of classic antiquity in our own universities." (*A Short History of Morals*, London, 1920, p. 86.)

36. We have the same testimony from Mr. G. K. Chesterton, who says " a real knowledge of mankind will tell anybody that Religion is a very terrible thing ; that it is truly a raging fire ; and that Authority is often quite as much needed to restrain it as to impose it." (*St. Thomas Aquinas*, London : 1933, p. 121.) Confucius, I think, knew this as well as Lucretius knew it eighteen hundred years ago (" tantum relligio potuit suadere malorum ") and as well as Whitehead and Chesterton know it to-day. Cf. above, pp. 86–7.

37. Eucken says somewhere " all specifically human achievement, *more especially ethical progress*, is an ascent from nature to spirit, an elevation of our being from the natural to the spiritual stage." This is a truth which

was perhaps discerned more clearly by Confucius and his followers than by Dr. Edkins.

38. Yet an Anglican bishop assures us that " if Communism fails in Russia—and I believe it will fail —the reason will be that it has dissociated itself from religion " ! (*Morning Post,* November 21, 1933.) Clearly, when we are told on the one hand that Communism is a religion, and on the other hand that it has dissociated itself from religion, the word " religion " is being used in two very different senses. What the bishop apparently meant was that the Russians have dissociated themselves from the *Christian* religion and have thereby sealed the doom of Communism. But what if Communism itself be a religion ? There is an interesting discussion of the question in *Modern Tendencies in World Religions* (London : 1933) by Dr. C. S. Braden, pp. 259 f. Bertrand Russell believes that " a full-fledged communist would say that Lenin is revered as the incarnation of a Force rather than as a concrete individual. He may in time become as theoretically abstract as the Logos." (*Sceptical Essays,* London : 1928, p. 225.) Something of the same kind might be said of Sun Yatsen in China, but his cult is not likely to survive the decay of the Kuomintang. With regard to the cult of Confucius, the Chinese have been remarkably successful in saving him from becoming either a " god " or an abstraction.

39. Although, as stated, Confucianism is neither atheistical nor materialistic, the Confucian School has always included atheists and materialists as well as

theists. One of the most noted of these was Tai Tung-yüan, who lived in the middle of the eighteenth century. He was one of those scholars of the Manchu dynasty who rejected the generally-accepted Confucian interpretations sponsored by the Sung philosophers, mainly because the latter had fallen under the influence of Buddhism and Taoism. The two hundredth anniversary of the birth of Tai Tung-yüan fell in 1924, and was celebrated with great enthusiasm in Chinese universities. Very numerous and laudatory were the books and articles about him which appeared at that time. His popularity among the " advanced " thinkers of the New China is largely due to his materialistic and anti-religious views, in which Young China finds satisfaction because they are believed to be in harmony with modern science. An interesting article on Tai Tung-yüan by Mr. Mansfield Freeman has been published in *The Journal of the North China Branch of the Royal Asiatic Society*, vol. lxiv (1933), pp. 50–71. Mr. Freeman observes that Tai Tung-yüan's philosophy is worthy of attention " because of the influence it has in current thinking to-day. Atheism is popular in modern China. This is partly a result of the study of contemporary philosophy of the West made by modern Chinese scholars and partly due to the atheistic teachings of Communism. An equally important reason, however, is the opposition to Christianity, because it entered China under the aegis of Western imperialism " (pp. 70–71).

For the general subject of " the strong anti-religious feeling " in contemporary China which is derived from

" anti-Christian feeling," see C. S. Braden, *op. cit.*, pp. 97 f. And see Pearl Buck's excellent remarks in her contribution to the volume entitled *Empire in the East* (New York : 1934), pp. 260–2. See also Dr. Hu Shih, *The Chinese Renaissance*, pp. 90–3.

40. Christianity is of course fully justified in calling itself a " Life " if only in view of the sayings, " I am the Way, the Truth and the *Life* " and " I came that they may have *life* and have it abundantly." Bishop Gore said that " Christianity is a life before it is a doctrine, and that life a fellowship." This is equally true of Confucianism with its closely-knit system of social relationships. But Christianity, if it is a Life, is also a creed, and we have it on recent episcopal authority that if Christianity be of this world it is also " essentially and primarily other-worldly." The Society of Friends has perhaps the best right of all Christian communities to say that religion is primarily not a creed but a Way of Life. (See Grubb's *What is Quakerism ?* London : 1917, p. 45.) To these remarks I will append a deeply interesting statement reported in the press to have been made in 1926 by James Waterman Wise, son of a Jewish rabbi in the United States, when he was giving up his rabbinical studies because he had ceased to be a believer in the Jewish religion. The Religion or the future, he says, " instead of beginning with the assumption of God and working down to man, will begin with man and human nature and end wherever man's highest nature leads. It will deal in human terms with human beings. It will busy itself with the earthly,

not the heavenly, springs of human conduct. Such religion will probably be without creed or dogma. But it will not be without life. For its very essence will consist of the essence of life. Its main purpose and ' excuse ' will be to help man to answer worthily the supreme question of his days : How shall life be lived ? With what aims ? By what standards, according to what plan ? The religion of the future will be in truth the science of life."

If that be so, we might almost be justified in adding that " the religion of the future " will be something very close to Confucianism. The same might be said of the " Faith of the New Republic " sketched by H. G. Wells in his *Anticipations* (Chapman & Hall, 1914, pp. 281 f.).

41. *The Philosophy of Plotinus*, 3rd ed., vol. ii, p. 164. The mention of Stoicism may remind us that we have in that great system another cult which, like Confucianism, was more than a system of ethics. Stoicism, as Dr. C. C. J. Webb has remarked, " was unquestionably a religion." (*The Hibbert Journal*, January, 1928, p. 353.)

42. *Texts and Pretexts* (London : 1932), p. 309.

43. *The Dance of Life* (Boston and New York : 1923), p. 3.

44. *Ibid.*, pp. 24, 25.

CHAPTER VIII

1. *Lun Yü*, vii, ch. xiii. (See Legge, *op. cit.*, vol. i, p. 199.)

2. *Lun Yü*, iii, ch. xxv. (Legge, *op. cit.*, vol. i, p. 164.)

3. *Lun Yü*, ix, ch. xiv. (Legge, *op. cit.*, vol. i, p. 221.)

4. *Lun Yü*, iii, ch. iii. (Legge, *op. cit.*, vol. i, p. 155.)

5. *Lun Yü*, viii, ch. viii. (Legge, *op. cit.*, vol. i, p. 211.)

6. *Mencius*, iv, pt. i, ch. xxvii. (Legge, *op. cit.*, vol. ii, pp. 313 f.)

7. *Hsün Tzu*, " Wang Chih Pien."

8. Confucius would have heartily disapproved of what Mr. Rutland Boughton defines as *antimusic*— " noises carefully or carelessly based on the inversion of natural musical law." He would have agreed that music " is not only a lovely thing in itself ; it is also an emotional record of real life." (*The Reality of Music*, London, 1934, p. ix.) The Chinese Sage would also have agreed with Mr. J. W. N. Sullivan (" But for the Grace of God ") : " One never realises the vulgarity of human beings so acutely as when listening to the mindless bawling of popular songs. . . . The latest type of popular music, jazz music, affects me as deliberately evil. . . . If our sociologists were also musicians they would find considerable social significance in the popularity of jazz."

In principle, as Mr. Ernest Newman has recently told us, there is nothing new in jazz or in the Western world's fondness for it. The " movement typified by jazz," as he says, " was known, *mutatis mutandis*, to the Romans, and was the subject of the wrath and sarcasm of the satirists. There comes a stage in an over-ripe

Q c

civilisation when, in sheer nervous exasperation, men revert to the mentality of a lower civilisation for novelty's sake and excitement's sake. In Juvenal's time the Romans were turning to Eastern music as Europeans now turn to jazz. . . . So let us take the philosophic-historic point of view with regard to ' music in decline.' There is nothing new under the sun." (*The Sunday Times*, May 20, 1934.) " Modern sociologists," as Mr. Peter F. Doran has said, " have failed to have regard for the relationship between music (instrumental and vocal) and political and social conditions. . . . We have accepted a new kind of music (crooning and jazz) and—it is more than a coincidence —personal liberty is being restricted ; such is Nature's revenge."

9. Jowett's *Dialogues of Plato*, vol. vi (" The Laws "), pp. 32 f., 179 f., 183, 474.

10. *Shuo Yüan*, ch. xix, p. 1 (*a*). Cf. also a striking passage in ch. xix, pp. 21 f.

11. *Rousseau and Romanticism* (Boston and New York : 1919), p. 211, note.

12. Cf. L. T. Hobhouse, *Morals in Evolution* (London : 1908), vol. ii, pp. 161–79, and the same author's *Development and Purpose* (London : 1913), pp. 114–15.

13. *Lun Yü*, bk. xi, ch. xxv, 7. (Legge, *op. cit.*, vol. i, pp. 247–8.) It is often assumed that Chinese music is *sui generis* and owes nothing to Western influences. It is doubtful whether this was true even of China's earliest ceremonial music, of which no trace is extant ; it is certainly not true of Chinese music as we know it

to-day. Those interested in the subject may be referred to an instructive article by Henry George Farmer on " Reciprocal Influences in Music 'twixt the Far and Middle East " in the *Journal of the Royal Asiatic Society*, April, 1934, pp. 327 f.

14. In one of its narrowest meaning *Li* is, indeed, " politeness." According to Mr. G. K. Chesterton " it is a pleasing thought that the word ' policeman ' and the word ' politeness ' not only have the same meaning, but are almost the same word." (*Illustrated London News*, March 24th, 1934.) Perhaps it is an equally pleasing thought that no Chinese would ever dream of associating *li* with policemen. According to Chinese ideas, a State governed by the principles of *li* would need neither policemen nor a penal code.

15. See the *Li Yün* (book vii of the *Li Chi*), section vi, 5. My quotations from the *Li Chi* (as from other Chinese classics) are in every case given in my own translations from the Chinese ; but for the convenience of English readers references are given to the volume and page of Max Müller's *Sacred Books of the East* in which Legge's versions are given.

Mr. Charles Duff in his book *This Human Nature* (London : 1930, p. 124) quotes the saying " ceremonies are the outward expression of inward feeling " and calls it one of " many profound mistakes." He would not have said so, I think, if he had examined the meaning of the Chinese word *Li* for which " ceremonies " (like Legge's " rules of propriety ") is a very inadequate translation.

Mr. Duff attributes the passage quoted by him to Lao Tzŭ, though it was Confucius and his School, not Lao Tzŭ, who emphasised the importance of ceremonial in a well-ordered State. Nevertheless it is recognised by Chinese scholars that there are parts of the *Li Chi* which are tinged if not saturated with Taoist influences, and this is particularly true of the *Li Yün* from which I have drawn some of my quotations. Dr. Legge, it may be remarked, observes that the *Li Yün* " bears important testimony to the sense of religion as the first and chief element of ceremonies, and to its existence in the very earliest times." (*Sacred Books of the East*, vol. xxvii, p. 24.)

16. *The Problem of China* (London : 1922), p. 190. For an equally serious misunderstanding of the same kind, see Kellett's *Short History of Religion* (London : 1933), pp. 440 f.

17. *Li Chi*, bk. xxv, sections 9 f. Cf. *Sacred Books of the East*, vol. xxviii, p. 275 and pp. 224 f.

18. *Yüeh Chi* (*Li Chi*, bk. xvii, *Sacred Books of the East*, vol. xxviii, pp. 93–115).

19. *Alexander's Feast*, two last lines.

20. *The Greek View of Life* (London, 8th ed., 1912), p. 212.

21. *Ibid.* It is not surprising that Lowes Dickinson, steeped as he was in Greek thought and ideals, became also a sympathetic interpreter of Chinese culture. That he had the temperament and the capacity to become so was evident to me when I met him for the first time during his only visit to China. In the summer of 1913 he

travelled from Peking to Shantung in the company of his friend, Dr. W. Perceval Yetts, now professor of Chinese Art and Archaeology in the University of London. I happened to be staying for a few days in a Buddhist monastery on the northern side of T'ai-shan, and it was on the pilgrim-pathway of that mountain that I joined them for a day. T'ai-shan, the holiest of China's sacred mountains, has been hallowed by ages of religious, artistic and poetic tradition. We spent the afternoon in a ravine, in a little pavilion at the edge of a mountain-stream, a spot that has been visited and loved by Chinese poets, artists, hermits and sages for hundreds of years. Lowes Dickinson's biographer tells us that " on T'ai-shan his feelings were definitely religious," and that this pilgrimage to the holy mountain was " the soul of his visit to China." (E. M. Forster's *Goldsworthy Lowes Dickinson*, London : 1934, pp. 149–50.) His own description of the visit occurs in his book *Appearances* (London : 1934, pp. 95–101). It closes with the words : " The West talks of civilising China. Would that China could civilise the West ! "

22. Legge translates " he listens to the singing of the Odes of the Kingdom and the Odes of the Temple and Altar." (*Sacred Books of the East*, vol. xxviii, p. 256.)

23. The last passage is taken from bk. xi of the *Li Chi*. (*Sacred Books of the East*, vol. xxviii. p. 18.)

24. *Yüeh Chi* (*ibid.*, pp. 128–9 ; cf. *Sacred Books of the East*, vol. xvii, p. 391).

25. *Mencius*, bk. ii, pt. i, ch. ii, 27. (See Legge, *op. cit.*, vol. ii, p. 195.)

26. *Li Chi,* bk. vii (*Li Yün*), *Sacred Books of the East,* vol. xxvii, p. 391.

27. *Li Chi,* bk. xi (*Sacred Books of the East,* vol. xxviii, p. 19). The pendants worn by princes and nobles varied according to their rank. The emperor's girdle-pendant consisted of pure white jade suspended by dark-coloured strings. Others wore blue jade with red strings, and so on.

28. I have rendered this passage from the *Chi I* (book xxi of the *Li Chi*). Legge's version will be found in the *Sacred Books of the East,* vol. xxviii, pp. 224–5.

29. See *Twilight in the Forbidden City,* pp. 171, 200 f., 308 f.

30. *The Greek View of Life,* p. 247.

31. W. Stade in the *Journal of the Royal Asiatic Society,* Oct., 1933, p. 1011.

32. William Watson, from " England my Mother " in *Lachrymae Musarum and Other Poems.*

Alfred Noyes, referring to the action of Shakespeare's *The Tempest,* says, very truly : " the suggestion in all this is not of a mechanically-worked universe, pulled by strings . . . but rather of a vast symphonic composition, in which the infinite subtleties and delicate adjustments may be likened to those of music, expressing the Supreme Will of the Master-Musician." (*The Unknown God,* London : 1934, p. 204.) The same eloquent writer tells us that when in youth he tried to picture the way in which " the vast system of law was actually used by the Supreme Power " he found that " the analogy of music always illuminated the whole matter." Every musician " knows that in his most intricate and subtle modulations he is doing something which somehow represents the way in which things may really happen. He is working out the golden mathematics of the process of wisdom whereby all things are ordered from end to end." (*Ibid.*, p. 103.) The analogy that music " offers us for the operations of the Spirit," he says, " touches with a universal significance the old legend of the city built to music. It makes us see, with Abt Vogler, how the whole fabric of the universe, and the walls and spires of the City of God, may be willed into being." (*Ibid.*, p. 104.) The true Confucian would have no difficulty in understanding the conception of the city built to music.

33. See Professor A. E. Taylor's comments on the Platonic theory of Music in his recent excellent translation of " The Laws of Plato " (London : 1934, Introduction, pp. xxiv f.) Confucius would doubtless have agreed with Plato that music is an " imitative " art, and that " it is essential to good music both that the object it ' imitates ' should be beautiful, and that it should imitate that object rightly. . . . The stipulation that the ' mood of soul ' which the music ' imitates ' must be genuinely beautiful brings in the moral side of the conception. To Plato, as a true Greek, the ' ugliness ' of conduct which is morally out of place is the most immediately salient fact about it, and the ' beauty of holiness,' if the scriptural phrase may be permitted, is something much more than a metaphor." Professor Taylor's further comment on this deserves attention.

" To judge by the tone of much of our literature," he says, " we are less sensitive on the point ; we seem slow to perceive ugliness in wrong-doing as such, or even ready to concede the ' artistry ' of great wickedness. It may be a wholesome discipline to consider carefully whether this difference of feeling may not be due less to a confusion on Plato's part between the beautiful and the morally good than to a certain aesthetic imperceptiveness on ours." (Taylor, *op. cit.*, p. xxvi.)

34. " The philosophy of the spirit tells us that the spirit desires three things and desires these for their own sake and not for any further aim beyond them. It desires to do what is right for the sake of doing what is right ; to know the truth for the sake of knowing the truth ; and it has a third desire which is not so easily stated but which I will now call the desire for beauty. . . . These three desires, and these alone, are the desires of the spirit ; and they differ from all our other desires in that they are to be pursued for their own sake, and can, indeed, only be pursued for their own sake. . . . So the spirit has three activities, and three alone, as it has three desires ; namely, the moral, the intellectual, and the aesthetic activities. And man lives so that he may exercise these three activities of the spirit, and for no other reason." A Clutton-Brock, *The Ultimate Belief* (London : 1916), pp. 20–1.

CHAPTER IX

1. " About 20,000 ' Marxist,' pacifist, Jewish or other ' un-German ' books, ' collected ' by the Nazi-led

students of Berlin University during recent days from public libraries and private owners, were burnt tonight in the Opera Place in Berlin in the presence of Dr. Goebbels, the Minister for Propaganda." (*The Times*, May 11th, 1934.) The matter of the book-burning in Germany seems to have attracted much less public attention than it deserves ; but an excellent article on the subject by Mr. Edward Crankshaw was published in *Everyman*, May 25th, 1934.

2. It was announced in the English press of April 9th, 1934, that a German library of the Burned Books was to be opened at 65, Boulevard Arago, Paris, on May 10th, the first anniversary of the burning. The establishment of similar libraries has since been announced in other countries. An exhibition of copies of the burned books was opened in Moscow at the end of March, 1934.

We see that what the " First Emperor " did in the China of the third century B.C. was, in principle, very much what Nazi Germany is doing to-day and what other countries, perhaps, will do to-morrow. He aimed at dictating to the people of China what they should and should not read. In June, 1934, the Press informs us that " the Nazi Propaganda Ministry have decided to dictate as far as possible the entire reading of the German public. Every month in future the Ministry will select six books . . . and recommend them over the wireless and in the Press as books which every patriotic German ought to be reading." (*Evening Standard*, June 14th, 1934.) The next step, presumably, will be to estimate the degree of patriotism attained by every

German by testing his knowledge of the books recommended and his ignorance of the books banned and burned.

3. Cf. the views of Mr. Ch'ên Tu-hsiu as stated by his friend Dr. Hu Shih in *The Chinese Renaissance*, p. 54. Among others equally zealous for " destruction " may be cited Mr. Ch'ien Hsüan-t'ung.

4. The term " crusade " is not such a misnomer in this connection as it may seem. The attack on Confucianism, as we shall see, was partly due to the direct or indirect influence of Christian missionary work in China, though the fiercest attacks on Confucianism in recent years have been made by non-Christian and often by anti-Christian Chinese.

5. This monthly periodical was published in Peking under the editorship of the president of the Confucian Association, Dr. Ch'ên Huan-chang. The article referred to appeared in the fourth number of the second volume.

6. *Lun Yü*, bk. ii, ch. xi (Legge, *op. cit.*, vol. i, p. 149), and *Chung Yung*, ch. xxviii, 1 (Legge, *ibid.*, p. 423).

7. Legge, *op. cit.*, vol. i, pp. 423–4.

8. Dr. P. C. Bagchi, in an article on " Chinese Mysticism " in *The Calcutta Review*, October, 1933.

9. See *Twilight in the Forbidden City*, p. 113.

10. *Ibid.*, pp. 153–4.

11. For an account of some of the activities of " the Christian General " see *Twilight in the Forbidden City*, pp. 376 f., 436–39 *et al.*

12. Some account of the affair was published in the Chinese press. An article on the subject appeared in the

Ta Kung Pao (the leading Chinese newspaper of north China) in its issue of July 16th, 1930. The damage done to the temple was fortunately not irremediable, and I understand that something has been done to repair it.

CHAPTER X

1. See *Twilight in the Forbidden City*, p. 22.

2. In spite of the high opinions of Confucian theory and practice held by some of the early Jesuit missionaries in China, the views expressed by their modern successors have been much less favourable. Even as a code of ethics, Confucianism is treated with scant respect. This attitude may with reason be attributed to feelings of hopelessness and discouragement in the face of the extreme rarity of genuine conversion to Christianity made among the Confucian *literati*. The modern Roman Catholic attitude towards the adherents of the Amidist and other Buddhist sects is more amiable than it is towards the less tractable Confucians —undoubtedly, I think, because conversions from Buddhism to Catholicism are much more numerous and satisfactory than those from Confucianism. The following quotation from Père L. Wieger's *Histoire des Croyances religieuses et des opinions philosophiques en Chine* (China : 1917) is very illuminating.

" Prise en masse, la classe lettrée est inconvertissable, à cause de ses vices honteux, de sa morgue stupide, et de son indifférence blasée . . . Je dis ceci de la masse. Dans le détail, il y a peut-être des exceptions. Il se peut qu'il y ait parfois des conversions, même complêtes. Mais la règle, si conversion il y a, c'est la conversion imparfaite, un reste du vieux levain demeurant toujours et fermentant à l'occasion. Mon expérience personnelle m'a appris, qu'un converti du Confuciisme reste pour le moins affligé d'un déficit ; de cette langueur qu'un mélange de rationalisme inflige toujours à la foi. Et le Chrétien chinois qui étudiera les textes de la secte, y brûlera les ailes de son âme, rampera désormais dans la *voie moyenne*, ne volera jamais plus . . . " Parlons maintenant du peuple illettré. Il est plutôt superstitieux qu'incrédule. La doctrine de la *voie moyenne* l'a fait minimiste et impulsif . . . Chez certains, toute aspiration religieux est étouffée par les soucis de la vie matérielle. Un petit nombre sont inconvertissables, par suite de leur attachement sincère à une religion hétérodoxe, Mahométisme ou Buddhisme. L'immense majorité est assex bien préparée à accepter le Christianisme, par un fond de foi théiste et de bonne morale, résultante hybride des diverses religions prêchées en Chine au cours des siècles. Les membres de certaines sectes religieuses, les Amidistes et les Tantristes . . . sont très bien préparés pour le royaume de Dieu " (pp. 699–700).

3. *The Chinese Classics*, vol. iii, part ii, p. 342.

4. *Reports of the Edinburgh Missionary Conferences of 1910*, vol. vii, p. 19.

5. *Ibid.*, pp. 92–3.

6. *Ibid.*, p. 20.

7. *The Rebirth of China*, p. 5.

8. *The Times*, April 26th, 1913.

9. *Edinburgh Reports*, vol. vii, p. 21.

10. *Ibid.*, p. 11.

11. *Ibid.*, pp. 95, 97.

12. It would, I think, be fairer to substitute " Protestant " for " Christian " in this and other paragraphs. So far as I have been able to ascertain, the Catholic Church in China has never allowed itself or its members to be drawn into the maelstrom of revolutionary agitation. The Chinese Christians who sprang into political prominence at the outbreak of the revolution were all, or nearly all, connected with Protestant denominations.

13. The two Houses of the Republican Parliament were opened at Peking on April 8th, 1913. The Cabinet issued the famous appeal for the prayers of Christendom about a week later. The question was not submitted to Parliament for discussion. April 27th, 1913, was the date appointed for the public prayers, and the day came to be known as " Prayer Sunday."

14. *The Times*, April 29th, 1913.

15. A missionary journal published a photograph of the Altar of Heaven and appended to it an exulting description of the Christian exploit and a prophecy of similar successes in a still more triumphant future. In a similar spirit, Christian missionaries who had been enjoying the hospitality of Buddhist monks in the Buddhist island of P'u-t'o (Pootoo) expressed the hope that this beautiful island, which had been consecrated to Buddhism for hundreds of years, would eventually become a stronghold of Christianity. (See my *Chinese*

Appeal to Christendom Concerning Christian Missions [London : 1911], pp. 75–7.) It may be mentioned that shortly after the episode of the Christian annexation of the Altar of Heaven, a group of students of the Y.M.C.A. held an athletic meeting there. (See *The North China Daily News*, October 25th, 1913.) For further remarks on the fate that befell the Altar of Heaven under republican auspices, see *Twilight in the Forbidden City*, pp. 110, 123, 204.

16. Readers of Chinese may find a full account of the activities of Mr. Chung Jung-kuang, and of the deep and very natural resentment caused thereby, among non-Christian Chinese, in the first number of the journal of the Confucian Association (*K'ung Chiao Hui*) published early in 1913.

17. See a letter by the honorary secretary of the Church Missionary Society published in *The Times* of April 29th, 1913.

CHAPTER XI

1. China. *The Quarterly Record of the Christian Literature Society for China*, July, 1913, pp. 662–3. It is interesting to note that one of Dr. Ross's fellow-contributors to the same number of this periodical was himself one of the earnest but ignorant missionaries to whom Dr. Ross alluded. According to Bishop Bashford, Confucianism had no message of any value for modern China ; its ethic was " sadly defective," and the bishop went out of his way to express doubts as to the sincerity and good faith of Confucius himself.

2. *The Chinese People* (London : 1914), p. 224.

3. *Ibid.*, p. 417.

4. *The Peking Daily News*, August 27th, 1913.

5. *China's Millions*, December, 1913, p. 188.

6. *Ibid.*

7. *The North China Herald* (Shanghai), December 6th, 1913.

8. For an estimate of the character of Yüan Shih-k'ai, see *Twilight in the Forbidden City*, pp. 35, 42, 101–9, 115–30.

9. *Ibid.*, pp. 126–7, 132, 163. Reference may also be made to my article in the *Quarterly Review*, Jan. 1927, on *The National Movement in China*, pp. 158–9. Cf. Dr. Hu Shih, *The Chinese Renaissance*, pp. 39, 55, 89–90.

10. See *The Autobiography of a Chinese Historian* by Ku Chieh-kang (trans. by A. W. Hummel), Leyden : 1931, p. 42.

11. *China's Millions*, December, 1913, p. 188.

12. *China*, No. 47, April, 1914, p. 726.

13. *Ibid.*, p. 731.

14. *Daily Mail*, March 16th, 1914.

15. See above, chapter x, p. 146.

16. It was a similar instinct of self-preservation that brought into existence a Buddhist Association for the defence of Buddhist interests. See my *Buddhist China* (London : 1913), p. ix ; and my articles on " The Religious Future of China" in *The Nineteenth Century and After*, November, 1913, pp. 910 f., and on "A Poet-Monk of Modern China " in the *Journal of the Royal*

Asiatic Society (North China Branch), vol. lxiii (1932), pp. 26 f.

17. It was published in two volumes by the Columbia University Press in 1911. The title of the book was ill-chosen, for it deals with much more than " economic principles."

18. Ma Ch'i-ch'ang, a well-known member of the T'ung Ch'êng School of Confucianism and a commentator on several of the canonical books such as the *Ta Hsüeh* and *Chung Yung*, died a few years ago, much lamented by Confucian China.

19. Among the works of Dr. Wilhelm which have been translated into English are *The Soul of China* (New York : 1928) and *A Short History of Chinese Civilization* (London : 1929).

20. The *North China Daily News* (Shanghai), August 26th, 1913.

21. See the *Reports of the Edinburgh Conference*, vol. vii, pp. 154–6.

22. Reference may also be made to *Buddhist China* (1913), pp. 6–11.

23. " The normal tendency of a bright young man is to rebel against authority. The opinions sanctioned by authority may be true or false, but once they are generally accepted, they will inevitably be defended by dull and conventional champions, and it is the triteness of the defence, rather than the principles involved, that is most obvious to the young. It is a mistake to assume that youth normally tends to advanced views. If the temper of the age favours advanced views, youth will

react towards orthodoxy, for youth always tends to criticise the prevailing shibboleths, whether they be the shibboleths of orthodoxy or of free thought, of conservatism or of communism. Garibaldi and Mussolini were both successful in their appeal to youth, though Garibaldi fought for freedom against the tyranny of the Church, and Mussolini for authority against the tyranny of the mob. And no doubt the coming generation will revolt against Fascismo when Fascismo ceases to be romantic and becomes merely respectable." Arnold Lunn in *Roman Converts* (London : 1924).

24. *The Church and the World in Idea and History* (Bampton Lectures : 1909), p. 289.

25. *The Book of Church Law*, by Dr. J. H. Blunt, revised by Sir W. Phillimore and G. Edwardes Jones, quoted by Walter Hobhouse, *loc. cit.*

26. Dr. B. S. Bonsall in his recently-published *Confucianism and Taoism* (London : 1934, pp. 63 *et al.*) takes it for granted that Confucianism was a State religion (in fact *the* State religion), and he describes it as such.

27. The article was published in the *Peking Daily News* of September 10th, 1913.

28. *Ibid.*

29. Dr. Georges Chatterton-Hill on " The Reawakening of France " in *The Nineteenth Century and After*, July, 1913.

30. Mr. T. S. Eliot and many other Christian writers argue eloquently that we should remain content with

Rc

our own tradition, not vainly try to adapt ourselves to that of an alien race and culture. But they fail to make it clear whether their advice that we should adhere to our own tradition is based on the fact that it is Christian, in which case it would surely clarify the issue if "tradition " were left out of the question and we were simply told to adhere to Christianity for its own sake ; or whether we are advised to adhere to Christianity because it is part of our tradition. In the latter case it would seem to follow that we should cease to urge non-Christian races to abandon their own tradition in favour of ours. (See *After Strange Gods*, London : 1934, pp. 48–9.)

Mr. Eliot tells us frankly that he personally could never make Confucianism a mainstay because *his* tradition is not Confucian. (*Ibid.*, p. 40.) The remark seems, in the circumstances, a very reasonable one. But he leaves us in doubt as to whether he would advise Confucians to abandon their own " mainstay " in favour of his. If he would, then it seems clear that his eloquent plea in favour of fidelity to one's own tradition is effective only if that tradition happens to be Christian.

Mr. G. K. Chesterton, writing recently of the hold that different religions have on different minds, said : " men will never entirely abandon what is at least relatively real : the traditions of their own fathers and the teeming vitality of the dead." (*Illustrated London News*, July 1st, 1933.) If that be true of Europeans—and Mr. Chesterton was referring to them—is it not equally true of the Chinese ?

31. Doolittle's *Social Life of the Chinese* (London : 1868), p. 608.

32. A. H. Smith's *Village Life in China* (Edin. and London : 1900), p. 349.

33. Cf. E. R. Bernard's *Great Moral Teachers* (London : 1906), p. 24.

34. See chapter i, note 1, p. 202.

35. " Yesterday idolatry, geomancy, *and the study of the Confucian classics* in elementary schools were, at a specially convened meeting of the village elders, officially abolished in the county of Ho-tsing. . . . The vested interests in temple property are too powerful to moulder at the first touch, but *this is nevertheless a tremendous step forward and a support to our evangel.*" The communication from which this extract was taken (the italics are mine) was addressed to the editor of a well-known missionary periodical and was described by the editor as " good news." (*China's Millions*, January, 1913, p. 13.) It will be observed that idolatry, geomancy and the study of the Confucian classics are all lumped together.

36. " China had been firmly anchored to the one idea that Confucius was right. *Now the whole philosophy of Confucius was upset,* not by the superiority of Christianity but by firm, hard facts which nothing could deny." (The Rev. Lord William Gascoyne-Cecil, now bishop of Exeter, as reported in *The Times* of November 1st, 1911.)

37. The Rev. C. C. B. Bardsley in *China*, July, 1910, p. 375.

38. His famous address on this subject was published as an article in the *Hsin Ch'ing Nien* (" La Jeunesse "), vol. iii, No. 6 (1017). Cf. Dr. Hu Shih, *The Chinese Renaissance*, pp. 90–1.

39. *Chinese Illustrated Review* (Tientsin), Feb. 18th, 1928.

40. *Ibid.*, March 10th, 1928.

41. See *The Times*, April 28th, 1927.

42. See above, p. 133. For my own contemporary account of the vicissitudes of Confucian fortunes during and after the period of the revolution of 1911, reference may be made to my article on " The Religious Future of China," published in *The Nineteenth Century and After*, November, 1913. I have borrowed from that article in the foregoing chapter.

CHAPTER XII

1. References to this movement may be found in K. S. Latourette's *The Chinese* (London : 1934, 2 vols.). In a review of this important work Mr. O. M. Green refers to the great significance of " the recent signs of a Confucian revival, so often coincident in Chinese history with a great period of national renascence."

2. I may perhaps be permitted to quote the following passage from my *Lion and Dragon in Northern China* (London : 1910), published less than two years before the overthrow of the monarchy, when signs of impending change were growing obvious to all. " That changes are urgently needed in certain directions goes without

saying ; but . . . it will be well for the stability of the
State if amid the contending factions into which the
intelligent sections of the country are sure to be divided,
there may always be one party in the land whose pro-
gramme will be summed up in the words ' Back to
Confucius ! ' That such a call will ever be literally
obeyed is quite improbable and certainly undesirable ;
but it is earnestly to be hoped that, however drastic
may be the social and political changes that China
is destined to undergo, her people may never come to
regard Confucianism, with all that the term implies,
merely as a fossil in a stratum of a dead civilisation "
(p. 449).

3. *North China Herald*, October 19th, 1932.

4. *Ibid.*, 1934. The article quoted, which is dated
February 14th, was presumably written by a European
missionary, for in Tachienlu there are no European
residents outside the mission-stations.

5. *Ibid.*, March 21st, 1934.

6. *Ibid.*, April 25th, 1934.

7. *Ibid.*, March 28th, 1934. The aims and activities of
the New Life movement have been described and discussed at great length by speakers and writers in China,
and references to its progress are to be found almost
daily in every good Chinese newspaper. Admirable
articles have appeared in the *Ta Kung Pao* (the leading
Chinese newspaper of north China), notably in its
issues of March 10th and 20th and April 1st, 1934.
The same paper in its issue of March 23rd published
a valuable essay on the subject by Dr. Hu Shih. One

of Marshal Chiang's speeches at Nan-ch'ang was fully reported in its issue of March 17th. Articles in the foreign press in China have naturally been less numerous and less illuminating, but a good English account of the movement appeared in *Oriental Affairs* (Shanghai), in its issue of May, 1934. In the course of this article occurred the following words. " Many of China's intelligentsia to-day frankly recognise that national salvation is not to be sought by what one of them has described as ' nothing more than depreciated currencies smuggled in from foreign countries ' which run counter to the spirit of the Chinese race. The New Life movement, starting with an attempt to improve the daily life of the individual, will if it can be made to conform to realities, hold greater promise than the fantastic political and social theories which from time to time have found support, especially among the younger generation. It aims at making a better citizen out of the individual, instead of infecting the masses with catchwords which are based upon exotic doctrines entirely alien to China's best traditions."

8. The phrase " Chinese Empire " (*Chung-Hua Ti Kuo*) was not known to Chinese constitutional law or theory. The official name of the Empire during the period of Manchu rule was *Ta Ch'ing Kuo*, signifying the Empire or State of the Ta Ch'ing dynasty. *Ta Ch'ing* was the dynastic title assumed (in imitation of Chinese usage) by the Manchu sovereigns shortly after they had established the independence of Manchuria in the first half of the seventeenth century and before

they penetrated the Great Wall and established themselves on the Dragon Throne at Peking in succession to the Chinese *Ta Ming* dynasty. It is therefore more accurate to speak of the Manchu Empire than of the Chinese Empire when we are dealing with the period 1644–1911. (See *Twilight in the Forbidden City*, pp. 112 f.)

9. Lytton Report (Series of League of Nations Publications, vii, Political, 1932, vii, 12), p. 99.

10. *The Book of Mencius*, bk. iii, pt. ii, ch. v (Legge, *op. cit.*, vol. ii, pp. 273 f.).

11. *Ibid.*

12. *Op. cit.*, vii. 1 (*a*).

13. Lytton Report, p. 93.

14. This appears to be the meaning of a difficult passage which has been variously interpreted.

15. My version of this famous passage is not identical with Legge's, which may be found in *The Sacred Books of the East*, vol. xxvii, pp. 364–6. It is a passage which has engaged the attention of innumerable commentators.

It is probable that the deep interest taken by Chêng Hsiao-hsü in the Confucian principles of *Wang Tao* was originally kindled by his brilliant contemporary K'ang Yu-wei, with whose writings and theories he was of course familiar. The following passage from Dr. Arthur W. Hummel's introduction to his book *The Autobiography of a Chinese Historian* (Leyden : 1931) will throw a light on the subject. " At a time when Darwinian ideas were almost unknown in China, he [K'ang Yu-wei] propounded what he believed to be the Confucian concept of *san shih* or ' three eras.' The first was an era of ' world confusion ' in which men must be governed either by force, or by rules of decorum to which they are expected to respond ; the second an era of ' advancing peace ' in which the masses are educated and share in governmental control ; the third an era of ' world brotherhood ' of which K'ang Yu-wei believed we have Confucius' own picture recorded in a famous passage in the *Record of Rites* [namely, the passage here translated]. In a later work, the *Ta T'ung Shu*, he outlined in more detail the social and political Utopia toward which society would move, hoping thus to make his ideas the rallying cry for national unification and a guiding-star toward social reform. But in demanding that his theories be linked with the personality of Confucius he unconsciously lifted them out of the field of history into the rarefied atmosphere of philosophy and religion. It is not surprising, therefore, that after the establishment of the Republic his views became the basis of a Neo-Confucian religious movement sponsored by his pupil Ch'ên Huan-chang." (Pp. xiii-xiv.) See above, pp. 157 f. For Ch'ên Huan-chang's own statement, see his book *The Economic Principles of Confucius and his School*, vol. i, pp. 15–22. He gives his version of the passage from the *Li Yün* of which I have given a partial translation, and describes it as " the most important statement of all Confucius' teachings." In support of the view that " World Brotherhood " is a defensible and appropriate rendering of " Ta T'ung," see Dr. Ch'ên's footnote on pp. 16–17. He rightly protests against the common Western view that Confucius made " no provision for the intercourse of his country with other and independent nations."

16. K'ang Tê is the *nien-hao* ("year-style" or " reign-title ") of the emperor, and replaced the year-style Ta T'ung on his enthronement on March 1st, 1934. " K'ang Tê " means " tranquillity and virtue," and the first character *k'ang* has a reference to the Confucian teaching that a period of *hsiao k'ang* (which Ch'ên Huan-chang translates or rather explains as the " Advancing Peace " stage) must precede the period of Universal Brotherhood or " the Golden Age of Confucianism."

17. *The Atlantic Monthly*, May, 1934.

18. See above, pp. 64 f.

19. See *The Individual and the Community*, by Wen Kuei Liao (London : 1933), pp. 286, 290. Cf. Dr. Sun Yat-sen, *op. cit.*, Lecture I, p. 8.

20. Those who are interested in this subject and cannot read Chinese should consult an excellent work in French by Dr. Yüan Cho-ying, a young Cantonese scholar. It is entitled *La Philosophie Morale et Politique de Mencius* (Paris : 1927). He claims Dr. Sun as " un défenseur de la doctrine confucéenne " (p. 18).

21. Cf. my *Ancient Chinese Philosophy* (Peking : 1923), reprinted from *The Chinese Social and Political Science Review*, April, 1923, pp. 8–10.

22. See above, pp. 123 f. Cf. Mr. Dudley Tyng's

article on " The Confucian Utopia " in the *Journal of the American Oriental Society*, vol. liv, No. 1, March, 1934, pp. 67 f.

23. See G. D. H. Cole in *What Marx Really Meant* (London : 1934).

24. See *God and the Astronomers*, p. 120.

25. Cf. p. 168.

26. It is disappointing to find so acute a thinker as Dr. W. R. Inge among those who have been moved to utter the trite remark that Christianity has not failed because it has never been tried. " Have we really any reason," he asks, " to be despondent, and to think that a religion which has never yet been fairly tried, has failed ? " (*Things New and Old*, London : 1933, p. 96.) Some years ago Dr. Inge made a similar remark in an article in *The Yale Review*. " It will be time to talk about the failure of Christianity when we have given the religion of Christ a fair trial. This we have never done yet on a large scale." No doubt this is true enough, but would Christians not do well to consider whether they are not too ready to talk about the failure of other religions without considering whether they have been given " a fair trial on a large scale " ?

27. Irving Babbitt, *Democracy and Leadership* (Boston and New York : 1924), p. 36.

28. *The Yesterday and To-morrow of English Poetry*, by Sir Henry Newbolt, C.H., Lewis Fry Memorial Lecturer, Bristol University, 1929–30.

29. See *Sacred Books of the East*, vol. xxviii, p. 259.

INDEX OF NAMES

GENERAL INDEX

For EU product safety concerns, contact us at Calle de José Abascal, 56–1°, 28003 Madrid, Spain or eugpsr@cambridge.org.

 www.ingramcontent.com/pod-product-compliance
Ingram Content Group UK Ltd.
Pitfield, Milton Keynes, MK11 3LW, UK
UKHW010347140625
459647UK00010B/886